Patients, Nannies, and Her Kids Agree: Carmen Teague Tries to Do It All

What Her Patients Say about Her:

I noticed Dr. Teague received a degree in psychology since the last time I came. That made me even more happy she's my doctor. I feel I can voice my concerns and she will genuinely be able to listen and voice her concerns. Love that she's a spiritual woman!

Dr. Teague is an exceptional doctor and human being. She makes the office visit a wonderful experience!

Dr. Teague . . . understands that treating the patient is about treating the whole patient, not just the specific symptom.

I am a Muslim woman in a headscarf. My doctor is a devout Christian. We are sisters! She always hugs me and makes me feel welcome. She is professional and culturally respectful.

What Her Nannies Say about Her:

Living with the Teagues is a real adventure. Carmen is the most multitasking person I've ever met, and yet she is able to do it all with love and excellence. A real-life inspiration of a wife, a working mom, and a Christian. Sharing life with her taught me that things don't have to be perfect to be amazing—it's all about how you deal with imperfection.

Being fearless and redeemed, Carmen Teague influenced me to be a better woman in three key ways: to love God above all, to give without counting the cost, and to have a crazy big family because those are the best ones.

What Her Kids Say about Her (No Bribes!):

My Mom is the best mom ever even though we sometimes can't decide which one of us knows everything.

My mom loves red lipstick. She never leaves without it. I love mom.

Mom is the strongest person I have ever met. She is still not in an insane asylum, even with all of us kids!

Loving, kind, cool, awesome. She makes everyone's day—if not, I don't know what does. She is the best mom in the world, Dr. Carmen Teague.

In Christ's love,

Carmen Teague

Motherhood, Medicine, and Mayhem:
A Doctor's Journey of Finding Calm in Chaos

by Carmen Teague, MD

FOUR T
PUBLISHING

Acknowledgment
"I Am a Promise," by Gloria Gaither and William J. Gaither. Copyright © 1975 Hanna Street Music (BMI) (adm. at CapitolCMGPublishing.com). International copyright secured. All rights reserved. Used by permission.

ISBN 978-0-9994302-1-7

Cover design: Diana Wade
Interior design: Diana Wade
Cover photo credit and back cover phot credit: Mike Newcomer

Four T Publishing
Charlotte, North Carolina
carmen-teague.com

Contents

Dedication:
To my Fabulous Family . . . you know who you are!

Introduction

Last April, I was at a women's retreat at Lake Junaluska, North Carolina, with a group from my church, Forest Hill Church. The speaker challenged us to do the thing that had been laid upon our hearts to do. I knew I had to write this book.

For several years, I'd had the opportunity to share this story, or parts of it, with various audiences, including professional colleagues, church groups, and patients. Over and over, people encouraged me to write my stories down. I laughed. Over and over, I laughed. I have no margin in my life for writing. I am no writer. As a physician, a health-care administrator, and a mother of four kids, I have no time. In fact, even at the retreat, I was reminded of the chaos and lack of empty space in my life. The speaker had encouraged us to unplug, to disengage, to free our minds from the everyday chaos of our lives so we could listen to what God had to say to us. I embraced this thought and turned off my cell phone. At the first break on Saturday morning, I decided to check in with the family by text, as I knew my husband, Joe, had the four kids at home and four ballgames to provide shuttle service to.

I wrote: *Raining here. Not sure if raining there. Not sure if games canceled. Hope all is ok.*

His quick response sent me into orbit: *All good. Two games canceled. We adopted a dog today.*

OMG! Whatever God was trying to tell me was lost for the

next six hours as I mulled over this news. We had tried the dog thing before. Twice, actually. The first time was when my girls were four and two. That golden doodle pinned my two-year-old and had to be "rehomed" with a family that could handle its aggression. We tried it again when the girls were six and three and the boys were almost one. That lasted less than a year, as that golden retriever had to be rehomed to my parents' house after she ate our deck. Literally, one board at a time, she ate our deck. I had still not recovered from that experience. In my opinion, we were not ready for a dog!

I responded to my husband with every church-retreat-appropriate emoticon I could find: *You had better be kidding. We have not talked about this.*

Radio silence for the next six hours. The next text I received was a picture of an adorable rescue mutt with a big bandanna tied around her neck that said *Adopt me.*

I learned over the next few hours that my ten-year-old daughter, Tattie Anne, had placed an "activity" on Dad's calendar for the weekend. Between all the games, they were going to an event called Pet Palooza, a pet fair of all the rescue shelters in the area. I could just imagine the scene. One softie dad walking around a pet fair with hundreds of wagging tails and slobbery greetings, and four kids begging to take one home. Yep, he'd caved. My family had adopted a dog without me.

There I was at my retreat, trying to get all spiritually recharged and enlightened, while my family was staging a coup in my absence. As I gave some more thought to what a book about my life would look like, two words came to mind. The first was *entropy.* According to Webster's, entropy is defined as: "Lack of order or predictability; gradual decline into disorder; the degree of disorder or randomness in a system; randomness, unpredictability, disorder." My jobshare partner pinned this term on me years ago. She laughingly says that entropy surrounds me. The second word was *mayhem*: "Chaos, disorder, havoc, pandemonium, commotion, madness." Yep. All those apply to me as well. I was retreating to find order, peace, and predictability, while my home was spiraling into disorder. Entropy and mayhem are my reality. Yet I long for certainty, calm, and composure.

I returned home from the retreat at four o'clock on a Sunday afternoon, and I was informed that we would be "interviewed" for our dog adoption at six p.m. Nice warning. The foster couple arrived right on time with a small, shaking dog that looked completely forlorn and petrified. After what felt like an hour of interrogation and house inspection (Really? It's a dog!), the foster family informed us that we had passed inspection, and we were deemed an appropriate placement for Ginger. Standing at our bar, the young lady just oozed and gushed about how much she appreciated our willingness to take in a stray, to avoid a "dog-factory breeder," to adopt a dog in need. About that time, my sons walked into the kitchen. They are both adopted, and neither looks anything like me or my husband. I smiled and said, "Lady, look around. This is not our first rodeo." She blushed and stopped her inspirational speech.

After we got over the dog drama, I sat down with my husband and told him about my retreat revelation that I should write this book. He looked and me and grinned. "I've been telling you this for years!" He reminded me that other people told me this all the time as well. I just hadn't been listening.

But, but, but . . . I still was not convinced. I already had no spare time. Now, we'd added a dog to the mix! The thought of writing a book was overwhelming. So I squelched it again.

Two weeks later, I had a work conference in Savannah, Georgia. In the middle of one of the sessions, I received a text from Joe: *In ten minutes, you'll get a call from a Tennessee number. Answer it. You won't be disappointed.*

Sure enough, 10 minutes later, the phone rang. It was Nancy French, who has written books with several well-known figures including Sarah Palin, Bob Fu, and Shawn Johnson. Somehow, Joe had connected with her via Twitter and convinced her to call and encourage me to write this book! She asked me if I was a writer. I laughed. And gave her a thumbnail version of my story. She simply told me that if I had been told to write this, I needed to do it! God would do the rest.

Still not completely convinced, I returned to work the next week and jumped into a crazy day of patient care, administrative duties, and the Teague household shuttle service. Midmorning, I encountered a new patient. When I was taking her social history, she mentioned she was an editor. I shared with her my recent musings over writing a book. As if God had placed her right there in the exam room, she told me exactly what I needed to do. I did not need an editor or a ghostwriter at this point. I needed a "book coach" to walk me through the process of writing, and she knew exactly to whom to refer me. Next thing I know, I'm sitting at a Starbucks with Betsy Thorpe, a literary specialist who had collaborated on several recent books, including *365 Nights: A Memoir of Intimacy* and *The Mustard Seed Chronicles*. Her first question to me was, "So, can you write?" I laughed. I had no idea. She simply said, "Send me what you have." Since the retreat, I had been jotting down ideas, mostly stream of consciousness, just trying to put into words the ideas that God has been churning in my head and in my heart for years. I lumped all the ideas into one big document and hit send.

Several weeks passed before I received her response. She didn't know it at the time, but I had thrown down the gauntlet with my submission to her—and the challenge was to myself. I had decided that her response would either make or break my writing endeavors. And it did: Betsy said, "You are a writer. You need to write this book."

Since you are reading this, I listened to all those voices. I took the challenge.

My story—this is it. Actually, it's not my story at all. It's the story of God weaving His grace and His mercy into and through a broken vessel. I've always loved the thought that light can only get out of the cracks of a broken vessel. I am definitely broken, but blessed beyond measure. I want to share my story so that others may be blessed as well.

Initially, I wasn't sure what the intended consequence was for writing this. Was it for me? Was God going to teach me something through the process? Or, was it for someone who might read it? Was there someone out there as stubborn and controlling as I am, who needed to hear my story? Were there others who need to hear that you can you have a life bursting with joy even when it does not go at all how you planned?

John 10:10 (The Message) says, "A thief is only there to steal and kill and destroy. I came so they can have real and eternal life, more and better life than they ever dreamed of." And Proverbs 19:21 says, "Many are the plans in a person's heart, but it is the Lord's purpose that prevails." Those two verses summarize my life. Nothing has turned out like I planned it. But this life that is so completely unpredictable, so far out of my control, is somehow more full than I could ever have imagined. Through writing this book, I have learned to embrace entropy and find meaning in the mayhem. Maybe, through reading it, someone else will learn to do the same.

1

Missionary to Medicine

*I praise you because I am fearfully and
wonderfully made; your works are wonderful,
I know this full well.*

Psalm 139:14

I love my job. Many people say that but don't really mean it. I do.
I get up every morning excited to go to the office to see what
opportunity awaits me to touch another life.

What do I do? I'm a doctor. So what does it mean to be a
doctor? Actually, I'm still trying to figure that out. Yes, I have an
MD behind my name. But that sorely fails to capture the privilege
I have of meeting people at their point of need.

I never wanted to be a doctor. In fact, I fought it with every
ounce of mental energy I could muster. If anyone had said to me
in grade school, or even college, that I would pursue a career in
medicine, I would have laughed in his or her face. Maybe my
journey to get here explains why I love it so very much. Or why I

cannot imagine doing anything else.

On the first day of school in fifth grade, my teacher asked us to go around the room, stand, and tell the class our name and what we wanted to be when we grew up. I, of course, popped up first, as I'm always a front-row-Joe kind of girl, and exclaimed, "My name is Carmen and I want to be a missionary when I grow up!"

The teacher had a look of bewilderment on her face. "Um, okay. What exactly is that?"

With my hand on my hip and my best matter-of-fact tone, I replied, "Somebody who tells the world about Jesus!"

By the fifth grade, because of my Southern Baptist upbringing and being at our church every time the doors were opened, I was very much immersed in the stories of missionaries who served around the world, like Lottie Moon, a young woman who had given her life to care for the people of China. It just made a lot of sense to me: if I was given to God for His purpose, shouldn't I be telling the world about Him?

Academics came pretty easy for me. Not that I didn't have to study, but I actually liked to study, and I loved to learn. I felt it was my responsibility to give everything I had: 100-percent effort, for the glory of God. I felt like my performance was not a reflection of me, but a reflection of God's gifts in me. One particular teacher imprinted this lesson on me—Ms. Morgan, my seventh-grade English teacher. After school one afternoon, when I am sure I had stayed to work on a project, she pulled me aside and asked me if I knew about the Morehead Scholarship. I had no idea to what she was referring. She explained me that it was an academic scholarship to the University of North Carolina, Chapel Hill. The scholarship valued academics, but also leadership, sports participation, community service, and moral character. She encouraged me to pursue my passions in all these areas, as she thought I might be a great scholarship candidate someday.

I am sure Ms. Morgan has since gone to be with the Lord and has no idea what a seed she planted in my life at that time. But she inspired me to give my best in every endeavor, not just academics. For years, I had heard the parable in John about the man with many talents, and thought maybe that was true for me. Now, Ms. Morgan had planted in my heart the idea of a scholarship and going to college without needing my parents to pay for it. I had no intention of ever going to Chapel Hill, as I was a Demon Deacon fan. However, if there was a scholarship like this at one school, there would surely be similar ones at other schools.

Senior year of high school rolled around, and I applied to as many schools and scholarship programs as I could. I wanted my parents to be free of the burden of paying for college. By this point, I was still headstrong on being a missionary, so I really wanted to go to a faith-based school. Wake Forest fit all my parameters. I had grown up Southern Baptist, and Wake had originally been a Baptist school. I had a pastor uncle who had gone there as well. I applied with fervor. At that time, you could not apply for the scholarship to Chapel Hill that had been mentioned to me by Ms. Morgan; you had to be nominated. Honestly, I was not that concerned about it, as it was specific to Chapel Hill, which I had no plans to attend. So, when I was nominated by my school counselors for the Morehead Scholarship, I was flattered. I felt like I had to give it my best effort through the interview process, even though my heart was still pulled to Wake Forest.

After making it through the local and regional interviews, I was invited to Chapel Hill for the finalist interview weekend. At that time, there were approximately 120 students from around the state and from select private schools throughout the country who came to Chapel Hill to compete for this scholarship. After several days of being wooed on this campus, I started having doubts about Wake because *this place was awesome*! But I was also utterly intimidated. For years, I had been a big fish in the small pond of Hudson, North Carolina. Suddenly, I felt like a guppy in an ocean of big-fish students whose life experiences so far exceeded mine.

The intimidation went into overdrive as I stepped into my final interview. That committee consisted of some of the most distinguished professionals and business people in the country. I walked into the room and sat down at one end of a very long table and saw Hugh McColl, then the CEO of NationsBank (precursor to what became Bank of America in 1998, one of the largest banks in the world), staring back at me. At that point in my life, although I knew I wanted to be a missionary, I had just returned from a mission trip to Paraguay. I thought I might be able to combine my desire to serve God with foreign diplomacy. (I admit, I look back on that thought now and laugh!) When asked about that trip, I answered the questions as best I could, but was startled with the response from across the table.

"Young lady," Hugh McColl barked, "I happen to be an international banker and travel to Paraguay frequently, and that country is nothing like you say it is." I smiled the most polite small-town smile I could muster, and asked gently where he'd traveled in Paraguay. Asuncion, the capital, he said. I replied that I had spent all my time in an area 250 kilometers outside of the capital and, I assured him, my experience was exactly as I had recounted.

He crossed his arms, leaned back, and glared at me from the end of the table. It was all I could do to choke down the tears welling up in my eyes. He continued his assault with more questions about Paraguay until his fellow interviewers intervened and stopped his tirade. I finally got out of the interview and went to the bathroom to compose myself. The next event after my interview was a luncheon with all the scholar applicants. I pulled myself together and went to find my seat. Just as the meal was being served, I felt a tap on my shoulder. It was Mr. McColl. "Young lady," he said, "before you pursue a career in that field, don't you think you had better learn a little more about it?"

I flashed my sweet-tea Southern smile and replied, "Well, isn't that what Chapel Hill is for?"

A week later, I received a scholarship and a personal congratulatory letter from Hugh McColl, including a two-year subscription to *Foreign Affairs* magazine. I think I read one issue and decided political science was not the life for me. Chapel Hill may not have been what I had planned, but it was exactly where God wanted me.

I always knew I wanted to help people, and I thought diplomacy would be that venue for my mission work. But after my first political science class, I decided that perhaps just listening to folks was a better option. Psychology sounded like the right choice. Of course, there was also a love of musical theater in my blood from my mom. So I doubled-majored, adding to psychology a performance degree in speech communications.

I loved combining music and worship, and missed the choir tours I used to take in middle and high school. When I looked around the massive campus at UNC and could not find an outlet for combining those passions, I dropped an ad in the *Daily Tar Heel* the first week of school my sophomore year, to see if there were any other Christian musicians out there who wanted to get together and play. The first person to call me was a fellow Morehead Scholar with whom I had shared a few classes as a freshman. In just a few weeks, we had created Heels to Heaven. This organization combined the best Christian music with a passion to share the gospel. We were basically a contemporary Christian praise choir that sang in churches, campuses, and various venues throughout the Southeast. It was an awesome experience. To my knowledge, the organization still exists on the Chapel Hill campus today.

The rest of my college memories are punctuated by the amazing summer experiences afforded to me by the Morehead Scholarship. The first summer, before I even started my freshman year, I completed an Outward Bound course in the southern Sierra Nevada Mountains in California. Twenty-three days carrying a sixty-five-pound backpack, including seventy-two hours of absolute solitude, will certainly challenge the limits of your physical and psychological stamina! I did experience my most embarrassing moment on this trip, at least the most embarrassing moment to that point in my life. About ten days into the trip, we set up camp one night at a place called Bear Crossing. You think that would have given us a clue as to the dangers awaiting. Appropriate camping technique is to hang any bags with food in them high in the trees, so that animals cannot access them. Furthermore, you're supposed to leave your remaining gear at the center of a circle with your sleeping bags arranged like spokes of the wheel. We had done all of the above, according to the book, and had just lain down to go to sleep. Of course, nature called, and I needed to go to the "bathroom." I wandered off just out of sight of my campers, and plopped down on the end of a log to do my business.

It was dark and I could not see well, so I was trying to hurry and finish. Mind you, toilet paper was not to be had on this trip, so I had learned that pinecones were the best apparatus to wipe the tush. I started groping around to find the sanitary object of choice, and I realized that I was not alone. At the end of the same log where I was sitting, there was a small brown bear. Actually, it could've been the size of Texas. I'm not sure. I just knew the log was not big enough for the both of us. I jumped up and ran back into camp screaming, "Bear bear, bear!" I was met with hysterical laughter—which didn't seem like an appropriate response to someone screaming, "Bear!" Within a few seconds, I realized that their laughter was because my pants were still at my ankles. Needless to say, the laughter scared the bear away, and I was left to sulk in my sleeping bag for the rest of the night.

My second scholarship summer was an internship with the Los Angeles Police Department. The goal of this summer experience was to get an appreciation for public service. And, boy, did I gain an appreciation—and an education. For a small-town girl from North Carolina, LA was shocking. Most of the time was a blur, rotating through the different departments in the LAPD, including CHiPS patrol, the K-9 units, and Homicide Investigation Unit. By far, my favorite rotation was with the Hollywood Vice Squad. We got to answer an alarm call at Madonna's home, where we were greeted with, "Sean, you better not be f#@$ing with me again!" We picked up Eddie Murphy, who was picking up drag queens. And we went on a high-speed car chase through the Hollywood Hills. Craziness. My favorite experience with that unit was a last-minute trip to go skydiving. Skydiving, really? But that's my attitude on life: you only get one shot to live your life to the fullest, and I had no idea if I would ever get this chance again. Two hours after the opportunity arose, I was jumping out of a plane above the Mojave Desert. Wow.

The next summer, I lived in Manhattan and worked for Aris Isotoner, which is a division of the Sara Lee Corporation. The goal of that summer was to give scholars an appreciation for a Fortune 500 company. I am not sure I learned much about the company, but I certainly got an education about life in the Big Apple. I lived with two roommates in a one-room flat above a bar, a block from NYU, and over the main subway stop for Greenwich Village. I worked nine to five and played five to nine! The TKTS booth in Times Square sold discount student tickets to any Broadway show available. I think I saw twenty shows that summer. Between the drama of the theater and the drama of life in the big city, by August I was well versed in the study of human emotion and behavior.

My last Morehead summer was by far the best. The opportunity that summer was for a scholar to go anywhere in the world and study any area of interest, as long as it was educational. So my friend who started Heels to Heaven with with me and I decided that we wanted to spend our last summer sharing Christian music in another country. We made a connection with Singapore Youth for Christ and put together a duet rock 'n' roll routine that we could share with schools throughout Singapore. I'm still not sure the Morehead Foundation knows that they funded a mission trip, but they did! One day, I walked into Singapore Youth for Christ and looked at a poster in the stairwell that had I probably walked by ten times by this point. On it was the paraphrased verse Proverbs 19:21: "Man may plan all things, but the Lord's will be done."

I smiled, and thought, "Wow, God, that sounds a lot like my life to this point." I had wanted to go to a different school, yet He had to change my passion to Chapel Hill in order for me to take advantage of the scholarship. I had wanted to go into international diplomatic relations, and here I was finishing up a degree in psychology and speech communications and thinking about pursuing a PhD. Plus, I had been convinced there was no room in my life for a boyfriend, and now I was engaged to my high school sweetheart, Joe, and planned to be married next summer. How cool!

How could I have known that that verse would be the theme for the rest of my life?

I came back to my senior year and started the process of applying to graduate schools. Joe was already out of school and working as an accounting intern. In the spring of that school year, there was another marker moment during a conversation that was probably forgettable to the other person involved. Throughout college, I had served as a leader in an Intervarsity Chapter, a Christian discipleship organization. At the end of a large group presentation one night, the speaker, Dr. David Chadwick from Forest Hill Church in Charlotte, North Carolina, stayed to talk to the leaders. He asked about our plans for the future and what God was doing in all of our lives. I told him I was planning to pursue a PhD in clinical psychology and go into Christian counseling. He encouraged me to look at Gordon-Conwell Theological Seminary, as they had just opened a campus in Charlotte and were offering a degree in Christian counseling.

The idea of getting a strong theological background before entering the spiritual wasteland of academia sounded appealing.

I researched the location, applied, and within a few weeks, I had been accepted into the very first incoming class at Gordon-Conwell Theological Seminary in Charlotte. I put the PhD applications on hold and decided that getting this master's degree would better prepare me for what I ultimately wanted to do.

It also gave Joe and me direction. We bought a house in Lincolnton, North Carolina, so Joe could commute to his job in Hickory and I could commute to Gordon-Conwell. The educational model at GCTS is to encourage full-time work while pursuing classes on the weekend. I landed an amazing job working as the Director of Children, Youth, and Outreach at a church in Lincolnton. My job at the church was pretty simple: I did everything the pastor didn't want to do. So I graduated on Mother's Day, got married on the sixth day of June (D-Day for anyone who remembers), and started seminary on the twenty-first of June. My job started one week later. I was well on my way to that career as a missionary counselor.

Nine months into the counseling degree at Gordon-Conwell, the school announced it would put all its efforts in Charlotte into the Master's of Divinity program, by far its most popular program. Thus, Joe and I found ourselves with a difficult decision. I could chuck all the classes I had taken thus far, including Greek Exegesis and New Testament, and start over somewhere else. Or I could try to transfer the classes to another school. Of course, there was no guarantee that would work. Option three was quitting our jobs, selling the house, selling our cars, putting everything we owned in storage, and moving to Boston to finish the degree at Gordon-Conwell's main campus. It didn't take a lot of praying for Joe to look at me and say, "I'm in—let's go!" So that's what we did.

Less than one year after marriage, we sold our first little house, sold our decent cars and bought junkers for city living, rented a U-Haul, and trekked to Boston.

Let's just say our decision was met with some turning of heads and questioning expressions. No one understood why we would start over. But we were young, we had no kids, and we thought this could be an amazing adventure. In fact, the Steven Curtis Chapman song "The Great Adventure" became our theme. All my scrapbooks from that season in our lives bear that name. We moved to Boston with no jobs. Yeah, you heard me, no jobs. We found housing by serving as estate keepers for a very rich family who lived near the seminary. Rent was free in exchange for housework. The house was a masterpiece. It was owned by a couple who founded a natural food company (years later, they sold it and it became what is now GNC). The problem was, they had come from very meager beginnings, and they were fiercely protective of what they had. If they left the house, they wanted one of us there.

This season in our lives was a humbling experience. I was cleaning toilets for rich people so that I could finish a master's in counseling, and Joe, who was now a CPA, could not find work in his field, so he took a job loading trucks for UPS in the middle of the night. Humility took on a whole new meaning during those years. Luckily, UPS paid for school, and Gordon had a two-for-one program. So Joe opted to take classes with me, since he had nothing else to do during the day. My sweet husband has almost enough classes to have a master's degree in theology as well. He did that for six months, until tax season rolled around.

The seminary experience was so enlightening. My Southern Baptist church experience had been great, but I had never really been in an ecumenical environment. I learned more about grace there than anywhere. There were professors and students from all over the world, representing multiple denominations, who came together to truly study what it meant to know the Scriptures and walk in faith. I'll never forget a prank that one of the New Testament professors played on one of the Old Testament professors. We came in one morning to a large, leather-bound book attached to the Old Testament professor's door. The title read, *Everything the Bible Says About Infant Baptism*. When he opened the book, it was blank! These godly men could banter with one another with truth and grace without being offended.

I was like a sponge. From my undergraduate studies, I knew many facts about psychological theories. I knew Carl Jung, and I knew Freud, and I knew Maslow. But I had never studied them through the filter of the Scriptures. I had a professor at Gordon by the name of Pablo Polischuk who also was on staff at the Harvard Medical School. He had a refreshing perspective on the study of these theories that made an indelible impression on me. For example, he would say that sometimes it's okay to "spoil the Egyptians of their gold to build a temple for God." It took me several months of study and contemplation to understand what he meant. Basically, if all truth is God's truth, then there are elements of truth in all the secular psychological theories. That's why people believe them and are drawn to them. Parts of Freud's and Maslow's theories reflected ultimate truth. Our task was to filter those theories through the Scriptures to determine what was a reflection of our fallen nature (original Sin) and what was a reflection of the image of God in all of us. I was enthralled. I had this overwhelming sense that we truly are body, mind, and spirit. That intricate design could only be a reflection of God's hand.

The last year of my training, I was assigned an internship to work at Tewksbury State Hospital, a Massachusetts state psychiatric hospital for the criminally insane and the indigent insane. This particular internship was by far the most rigorous and least popular among the seminary students. It was very much a secular setting working with hard-core psychiatric patients. Furthermore, the internship preceptor at the site had a reputation of being quite nasty. The internship assignment was fairly random, but I had hoped NOT to be chosen for this one. But of course, such was my lot.

The facility was an old polio hospital that the state had transformed into a psych ward. And when I say psych ward, I mean the patients there were crazy, in the purest sense of the word. We had three Jesus Christs and four Virgin Marys on the same lockdown unit.

For the first three months of the internship, my goal was to serve as a faithful psychology intern on a multidisciplinary psychiatric team. I desperately sought to avoid the psychiatrist who headed our treatment team—I was scared to death of her. One day after we'd sat through multidisciplinary rounds and were mulling over how to best serve the patients in our care, my supervisor pulled me aside and asked me why I was wasting my life.

I was flabbergasted. I knew I had been working diligently to pull my weight on the team, and I had no idea what the basis of her critique might be. She said that she had been watching me, and that I had a knack for understanding the biochemical and physiologic abnormalities that our patients shared in struggling with their mental illness.

She said I needed to go to medical school.

I was so upset; I have no idea how I responded to her that day. I remember coming home and telling Joe what she had said. He looked at me intently and left the apartment for about fifteen minutes. He came back, looked me straight in the face and said, "Carmen, I think she is right." Now I was just mad. How dare she say this to me, and how could my dear soul mate think she could be right? They were both wrong, and I was going to prove it.

Joe and I had already started the process of applying to graduate programs. Joe had always wanted to go to law school, but had put that desire on hold to support me through seminary. I wanted to pursue my psychology training with a PhD. Because we were tired of the cold weather and snow in Boston, we picked ten cities south of the Mason-Dixon Line that had both a law school and a psychology doctorate program. Over the next four months, we eagerly awaited acceptance letters to programs so that we could make plans for our next move. Week after week, Joe got acceptance letters to law schools. And week after week, I got rejection letters from PhD programs.

I gradually fell into a deep, dark place. *How could this be happening?* Joe, who had played baseball in college and been less interested in academics than extracurricular activities, got accepted to every program, while I had never made anything less than an A in my entire life. I had a pristine academic record. I had been a Morehead Scholar, for heaven's sake! Yet I was rejected from every PhD program to which I had applied. I was devastated. And I was mad. My entire plan for my life was falling apart.

I knew from a young age that I had been called to be a missionary—or someone who told about the amazing life you could have in a relationship with an amazing God. I loved people, and I loved listening to them and understanding the intricacies of their lives. Christian counseling was a natural fit to combine both of these passions. But now I was being told no. Somehow, all my work to this point was just not good enough to get me the degree I needed.

St. John of the Cross was a sixteenth-century Spanish Catholic mystic. He wrote a poem entitled "The Dark Night of the Soul," which explores the painful experiences people endure as they grow in union and maturity in their relationship with God. This season was my dark night of the soul. As one stanza notes:

> *And in the luck of night*
> *In secret places where no other spied*
> *I went without my sight*
> *Without a light to guide*
> *Except the heart that lit me from inside*

As I worked through the rejections over the next few months, I resolved that I needed to try again to get into a PhD program. Joe chose to pursue his law degree at the University of North Carolina at Chapel Hill. That choice alone was a dagger to my soul—my alma mater! It just wasn't fair that he would be the one in school. But I owed him the favor of supporting his education this time. We had to eat, so I sought a job working in the field in which I was now trained. I started working at Duke University in Alzheimer's research. As a Tar Heel, it took a lot of pride-swallowing to work for my archrival.

The summer after seminary graduation and before law school started, we found ourselves without a place to live. We had to move out of the seminary housing at graduation. We could not yet move to Chapel Hill, as leases did not start until the fall semester. We ended up moving in with my grandmother, who was in the early stages of Alzheimer's and needed some in-home care. I thought this would be a good introduction for my job at Duke anyway. Since my job had not yet started, I took the opportunity to retake the GRE. I was convinced the reason I had not been accepted into a PhD program was my less than perfect score on that standardized test.

At the test-administration site, a local community college, the day of the test also happened to be a day of registration for summer school. Out of sheer spite, and to prove to everyone around me that the medical school idea was bogus, I signed up to take anatomy and physiology in summer school. I had never taken either in high school or college, and I was sure I would hate it, thus proving to everyone that medicine was not for me. Well, that's not what happened. I aced the GRE that day, but no one ever saw those scores.

We moved to Chapel Hill. I started work, and Joe started law school. I still was not convinced that medical school was in my future, but I was at least willing to entertain the thought. The next hurdle was organic chemistry. I had never taken it, or any chemistry classes, for that matter. I knew that organic chemistry had been the make-or-break class for all my premed friends in college. I even remember the class name: Chemistry 61. It had turned more than one of my classmates away from careers in medicine. Maybe this one would relieve me of this burdensome medical school idea as well. I looked into classes at Duke, Chapel Hill, and NC State. No one offered the classes at night; I had to take them at night because

I had to work. We had to eat.

I took this setback as an indication that I was not to pursue this path. Then, on the way to work one morning, as I was aimlessly flipping through radio channels, I heard an ad for Durham Technical Community College, "Now offering pre-med classes." *No way!* I called, and within a few days I was registered for organic chemistry night classes. In a week, I found myself sitting in an organic chemistry class with the former head of organic chemistry from UVA. He had recently left his position at UVA to take a research position at a pharmaceutical company in Research Triangle Park! What an experience! Every evening when we came to class, he simply asked us what drug we wanted to make that night. I was enthralled with organic chemistry. (Yeah, I know, enthralled with O-chem. Call me a nerd.) So instead of turning me away from medicine, that class pulled me in.

Within a year, I had applied to and been accepted at several medical schools. Of course, I chose Chapel Hill, and matriculated into medical school in the fall of 1997, five years after finishing my undergraduate education. Somehow my missionary path had morphed into medicine.

Few people would say that they had a spiritual experience in medical school. For the first two years, you sit in a classroom and try to imbibe knowledge from a firehose in a shot glass. I remember that I flunked my first cell biology exam. I was devastated. I did not know how to study, at least not for a multiple-choice exam. For the first twenty-six years of my life, I'd been able to get by on essays and fluff. This was different. In my psychology and humanities classes, there was always more than one way to get to an answer. In medicine, I began to think that there was only one answer to how the human body worked. And then that façade began to break down.

In the same cell biology class, we studied things like the Krebs cycle and coagulation cascade. I remember meticulously learning every step of the cascade or the cycle and getting to a point in the process where the professor couldn't explain it. He would gloss over it and keep going. All I kept thinking was: there is a huge leap of faith here. There must be intelligent design. My genetics and embryology classes were by far the most eye-opening. I remember learning the sequences and codons of DNA. I was fascinated seeing the helices come together in a clear and meticulous pattern. And I was overwhelmed by the thought that DNA is a language.

Right there, in the front row of my genetics class, I clearly heard God speak to me the words from John 1:1: *In the beginning was the word, and the Word was with God, and the Word was God.* As my professor tried to break down all of life into a language such as DNA or RNA, all I could think of was how God was the sustainer and creator of that language. He is the Word. That was a truly special moment for me. I had heard that scripture from the Psalms about how we are made. But it became so real to me through studying His creation.

> *I praise you because I am fearfully and*
> *wonderfully made; your works are wonderful,*
> *I know this full well.*
>
> Psalm 139:14

When the classroom work ended, I started my clinical rotations and became even more convinced that this was my calling. As a medical student, your job is to observe and learn. You don't have a lot of responsibility for making clinical decisions. You do, however, have a lot of time to talk to patients and hear their stories. Often, the medical student's job is to take a history and physical or to give instructions around discharge. I didn't know then how precious that time with the patient is. I rotated through every specialty—surgery, pediatrics, internal medicine, orthopedics, neurosurgery. I'll never forget the experience of having AC/DC's "Back in Black" blaring in the operating room as I helped saw open a person's skull. Neurosurgeons are a different breed.

The goal for this broad exposure to different medical specialties is to help medical students choose one for their field practice. I walked into medical school thinking that I would do family medicine. I loved seeing folks along the continuum of life. But I came to realize that although I love children, I could not stand seeing parents make poor decisions for their children. When I wanted to slap the parent blowing cigarette smoke in the face of a child with asthma, I decided pediatrics was not for me. In the same way, I realized I really did not like pregnant women. The hormonal chaos of a pregnant woman was more than I could bear. And delivering unwanted children to undocumented and underage moms was a heart-wrenching experience. Thus, I gave up the notion of family practice, as that would include both pediatrics and obstetrics.

I was left with my love of adults of all ages; internal medicine seemed to be the best fit for me. Those years working with Alzheimer's research had a profound effect on me, as I love spending time with men and women from whom I can glean much wisdom. And in working with critically ill patients and managing chronic disease toward the end of life, I realized that our medical ethics often fail. Just because we can do something does not mean we should do something, especially at the end of life. Quality of life and quantity of life are not the same. This was my mission field.

I was so convinced of this, in fact, that I did my honors thesis on end-of-life issues. I had the opportunity to study the medical literature filtered through the Scriptures and my faith-based appreciation of the sanctity of life. As a senior in medical school, I felt like I was in seminary all over again. Funny how things come full circle.

Yes, I am a doctor. But really, I am on a mission of helping us discover how we are fearfully and wonderfully made. Never in a million years would I have imagined that my mission field would be a ten-by-ten examination room. But it is. And it is beautiful.

2

Lay the Foundation

Love the Lord your God with all your heart and with all your soul and with all your strength. These commandments that I give you today are to be on your hearts. Impress them on your children. Talk about them when you sit at home and when you walk along the road, when you lie down and when you get up.

Deuteronomy 6:5–7

I was born in a fabulous small town called Hudson, North Carolina. I was blessed enough to be born into the church. And when I say church, I mean the body of broken believers here on this earth who gather to live out our purpose as agents of hope in a fallen world. My earliest memories are from the Southern Baptist Church, where my family attended. My mother and father married in that church at a fairly young age, and I cemented their marriage about a year later. They met in the church. I don't think they knew each other very well, but my dad had been my mother's bus driver in high school. She used to joke that she talked to him about her boyfriend problems. Then he became her problem, permanently! Apparently they connected around the fact that their fathers had died fairly young. My mother was nineteen when she lost her dad, and my father had lost his when he was about twenty.

My father never went to college because he had to stay home and support his mother. He went to work in a furniture factory and worked his way into factory management and stayed there for eighteen years. Around the house and at work, he was the handyman who could fix everything. His propensity to problem-solve and fix things led him to excel in the manufacturing world. My mother was fortunate enough to go to college on a veteran's scholarship and study teaching. (Her father had served in World War I. Let's just say she was a whoops when she came along to parents who were aged forty-four and fifty-five.) Her siblings were fourteen and fifteen years older than she, so she had two sets of parents—the real ones and her older brother and sister. My uncle always said she was a crybaby and a brat. Somehow, however, the crybaby and the handyman found each other and created me.

So, obviously, my two grandmothers attended the same church. I have vivid memories of sitting between the two of them on Sunday mornings. I can still hear their trembling voices singing the old hymns, "Just As I Am without One Plea" and "Leaning on the Everlasting Arms." Some of my favorite memories were seeing my mother's glare from the choir loft as one of the grandmothers unwrapped peanut butter and crackers in tinfoil for me and my little sister to munch on in church.

The Bible came at me from all directions, and I loved it. As a good Southern Baptist kid, I went to Wednesday night dinners, Mission Friends lessons about missionaries, and Sunday school.

Basically, I was there every time the doors were open. When it came to "drawing swords" (in which two players hold a Bible face-up and race an opponent to find Bible verses), I was a champion. My nemesis was the preacher's son, Jeff. He could find a verse almost as fast as I could, and I was determined to never let him win. I have great memories of those verses and of seeing them lived out in front of me.

And let us consider how we may spur one another on
toward love and good deed, not giving up meeting together,
as some are in the habit of doing, but encouraging one another.

Hebrews 10:24–25

Church was more than a place to us. It was our family. It was the center of social interactions. I knew everyone, and everyone knew me. My father drove a church bus and was intimately involved in the ministry that sought to bring children to church who otherwise would not go, as their parents did not go. I got up early every Sunday morning and went with him to pick up the "bus kids" and bring them to church. It was my job to hand out the candy.

I remember standing with these godly men who drove the buses every Sunday morning, and listening to them pray for these kids and for their hearts. I prayed right along with them. Then, we rode in the rickety old church buses into the trailer parks in our area. I don't think I ever realized those kids were different from me. I just thought their houses didn't look so great. I had a profound sense that God loved them and me just the same. They were kids like me. And we all loved candy. Every Sunday when we took them home from church, they got a huge handful from me!

*They devoted themselves to the apostles' teaching
and to fellowship, to the breaking of bread and to prayer.*

Acts 2:42

We had this breaking of bread thing down as well. You've not lived until you've been to a Southern Baptist potluck. You cannot imagine how many ways you can cook green beans, sweet potatoes, and squash. Did you know that you can put pineapple, crackers, and cheese into a casserole and call it a vegetable? Go figure. On those Sundays, the kids on the bus stayed and ate with us. We roamed around the graveyard, playing hide-and-seek. I know that sounds a little morbid, but it was so much fun. I figured that all the folks in the graveyard were dead, and they didn't care if we were running around the flowers and the gravestones. If it was a really special day, we would have homemade ice cream after church. I can still hear the grind of all those electric motors and hand churns as the little old ladies competed to see who had the best recipe.

I really looked forward to a special week in the summer called Revival. Revival was a BIG DEAL. For me, it meant going to church every night, Sunday through the next Sunday, with a meal there each night. A guest speaker came to talk (not the typical preacher) and the music was awesome. There were crafts that involved Popsicle sticks, tin foil, pinecones, and peanut butter. And the best part was that I got to sit between my two grandmothers, who brought me snacks every night. My mother was always up there on the platform, either leading the choir or singing right along with it. My dad was always in the back row, because he had to sneak in and out to handle the buses, or run the sound system, or fix whatever technology needed his assistance.

In addition to Revival, there was another week in the summer of my youth that I anticipated all year—Youth Choir Tour. Every year, our church youth group went on choir tour throughout the Southeast. During those years, we had an amazing youth minister who introduced me to the world of worship, music, and discipleship combined. Let me tell you, I could belt out some Sandi Patty and Steven Curtis Chapman, even in grade school! Of course, my parents were always chaperones on these trips, because that was just what they did. My dad drove the bus, and my mom helped manage the chaos on the bus. My little sister tagged along as the choir tour mascot. I can still see my father sitting in the front row of all the churches we visited, just weeping as we sang. It was a beautiful sight. That youth minister instilled in me a passion for worship, and he planted in me the notion that how we lived our lives could be an act of worship.

> *Therefore, I urge you, brothers and sisters,*
> *in view of God's mercy, to offer your bodies*
> *as a living sacrifice, holy and pleasing to God—*
> *this is your true and proper worship.*
>
> Romans 12:1 (NIV)

I memorized the translation above, but I've come to love and appreciate The Message translation:

> *So here's what I want you to do, God helping you: Take your*
> *everyday, ordinary life—your sleeping, eating, going-to-work,*
> *and walking-around life—and place it before God as an offering.*

Embracing what God does for you is the best thing you can do for him. Don't become so well-adjusted to your culture that you fit into it without even thinking. Instead, fix your attention on God. You'll be changed from the inside out. Readily recognize what he wants from you, and quickly respond to it. Unlike the culture around you, always dragging you down its level of immaturity, God brings the best out of you, develops well-formed maturity in you.

Romans 12:1–2 (The Message)

When you use the gifts God has given you, it is an act of worship, and it brings glory to Him. I saw this and experienced it growing up in the church, and I realized just how awesome it was that I knew I was part of a larger community that did not always go to church (like the bus kids). But I knew we were supposed to change the world around us for the better. If that meant handing out candy, singing songs of worship, or visiting local nursing homes with homemade cards and flowers, it was significant. It was worship. It was transformative for both the giver and the receiver.

*Seek ye first the kingdom of God,
and all his righteousness and all these things
will be added unto you.*

Matthew 6:33 (King James Version)

As a child, I remember learning the verse above. But more importantly, I remember seeing it lived out in front of me, especially in my parents. My parents were not perfect. I probably learned the best curse words from my father. He didn't talk a lot about spiritual things, but the tears streaming down his face when he saw me sing a worship song in church, or his simple prayers standing around with the men in the bus ministry, said more to me than any sermons. My dad's spiritual gift is service. He's a fixer and a doer. I saw him give to people in our community all the time. In fact, he gave away more than one car when I was growing up—sometimes leaving our family with one that did not run, or run well! I remember getting phone calls at three o'clock in the morning, letting him know the furniture plant he managed was on fire (again). Or that an elderly lady at the church, who lived in a trailer, had no heat nor hot water. To Dad, if there was someone in need, he never complained; he just went to help.

My mother, Carolyn, was the fireball in our house, and utterly and completely in charge. I give her the credit for being the spiritual leader, at least verbally. She's amazingly talented: a teacher, a writer, an artist, and an actress. Everything she touches she makes a little better. And she loves to serve. If there was ever an event that needing planning, Carolyn was asked to do it. Every year, my church did an Easter musical and a Christmas musical with the children's ministry. My mother produced the entire thing, top to bottom, from costumes to lights, from elaborate sets to special effects. It was truly amazing! I remember standing on an eight-foot ladder wearing a star costume holding my arms out to the side to the point where I had no feeling left in my fingers. However, every time I looked down at my mother, where she was directing from the front row, she glared at me to keep my arms straight. Needless to say, I made it through the whole production, still shining.

My parents' witness said it all to me. They poured their lives out to the people around them constantly, and with reckless abandon. It was the only example I ever knew. I knew that they understood "seek ye first," even to the point of need.

One of my favorite Christmases illustrated this verse more powerfully than any words. My father worked in the furniture industry, but that year he had shifted jobs in the company several times, and I don't think there had been a steady revenue stream coming into the house. As the holiday approached, my parents said multiple times that they did not want us to be disappointed at Christmas. They wanted us to know that we were "buckling down" and trying to be good stewards of all that God had given us. Yet we continued to see our parents give their money, time, and talents to the church.

On Christmas morning, my sister and I jumped up as always and ran into the living room, where the family Christmas tree stood. Although we were not allowed to touch a present until we read the Christmas story from the book of Luke, we were already summing up the loot under the tree: there were only two boxes. I hope my face did not show it, but I was probably a little disappointed.

After reading the story, our parents gave each of us a box to open. Inside, we found a pair of footed pajamas. Again, not what we were expecting. Mom and Dad instructed us to put them on. Even at age eight, I thought this was a rather odd request, as we were already wearing our nightgowns. Nonetheless, we put on those fuzzy PJ's. Then our parents said that they had one more present to show us. They led us into the backyard with our eyes closed. When we opened them, before us stood the most amazing Christmas present ever—a trampoline! Our parents had been able to scrounge up enough money to buy us one fabulous present. For hours that Christmas, we jumped on that trampoline in our footed pajamas. I even remember our aunts, uncles, and cousins jumping in as well.

That verse continued to ring in my head. As I've gotten older, I've studied the context of that simple verse that I memorized. Matthew 6 has several themes that my faith heritage taught me. First, my parents gave their resources away without any pomp and circumstance.

> *But when you give to the needy,*
> *do not let your left hand know what your*
> *right hand is doing, so that your giving may be in secret.*
> *Then your Father, who sees what is*
> *done in secret, will reward you.*

Matthew 6:3–4

My parents had faithfully given to others and, in doing so, had been able to provide the most amazing Christmas present ever to their kids. As a kid, I saw them bless so many others around them. They did not store up for themselves treasure on earth; they gave of what that had to others. My parents always said that they made memories for us, not dowries. For that, I am so thankful. My parents did not worry; they just trusted God would provide.

> *So do not worry, saying, "What shall we eat?"*
> *or "What shall we drink?" or*
> *"What shall we wear?"*
> *For the pagans run after all these things,*
> *and your heavenly Father knows that you need them.*

Matthew 6:31–32

My parents always said, "Give to God what was His first, and all other things will be supplied for us." I saw this. I lived it. Money, stuff, time, and talent. It did not matter. All of life was to be given away. It's what I want as my epitaph: *She held on loosely.*

———

Did we have daily devotion in my house? No. Did we have scriptures plastered all over the walls, mirrors and windows? No. Did we display "godly behavior" all the time? As my father would say, "Hell, no." But did my formative years teach me to love God with everything in me and hold on loosely to everything else? Hell, yes!

3

The Best-Laid Plans

Many are the plans in a person's heart,
but it is the Lord's purpose that prevails.

Proverbs 19:21

When I went on a blind date in high school with the boy who became my future husband, Joe, I remember being impressed by what he said about adoption: that it was a beautiful picture of God's grace, and that he wanted that for his life someday. I remember thinking, "Wow, this guy is deep. Maybe I should keep him." So I did!

Fast-forward ten years. Many of us make plans around when we think we will have children. I always thought I would have children about five years after marriage, but at our five-year mark, I was applying to medical school. It didn't seem like a great time, so we pushed the snooze button on fertility. The alarm went off again at the end of medical school. In fact, I arranged my classes so that I could have five months free between the end of my fourth year of medical school and starting residency.

I'm a planner. I bought ovulation kits. I counted days. I was bound and determined to conceive within that three-month window so I could have an adequate maternity leave before starting my residency. Exactly nine months prior to the last possible month that I could give birth within my amazing plan, I was doing a rotation in western North Carolina with a wonderful, godly woman named Dr. Jane Kirkpatrick. She had just come back from a mission trip and was exploding with the details of how God had worked through her and how she could not wait to get back to India.

While I was there, I ovulated, so I called Joe to meet me at a Motel 6 almost exactly halfway between his location in Chapel Hill and my rotation. Romantic, right? Backing out of Dr. Kirkpatrick's driveway and rolling down the window to make sure I didn't fall in a ditch on the left side, I clearly heard a voice say to me: "Carmen, you're not going to have a baby now. You need to go to the mission field for Me."

I rolled up the window thinking, *Really, God, did I have to roll down the window to hear that?* I skipped the Motel 6 and went back to Chapel Hill and told Joe that the timing was not right. He agreed, and we gave up our efforts. A few weeks later, the opportunity presented itself to travel to Kenya with World Medical Mission. I even had the privilege to travel with a couple from my church in Chapel Hill. I took those ditch directions to heart. I spent the next two months serving the Maasai people of Kijabe, Kenya.

The fertility alarm did not go off again until the middle of my residency. I realized I was thirty-two years old and my eggs were aging. Joe and I had been married for eleven years, and five years after our first efforts, we finally decided to try to have children again. We tried in earnest for months before we realized that we were struggling with infertility. I went through all the expected feelings: *What is wrong with me? Why did I wait so long to have children? Why did I put my career first and now have "rotten, old eggs"?* It was an agonizing and frustrating process. I was completely riddled with guilt. My dad asked if he needed to draw a diagram for us of how to have a baby. Six months of Clomid and three rounds of intrauterine insemination yielded nothing. In my doctor's infinite wisdom, he asked us to take a month off from trying. Making a baby on demand is a stressful process. The next month, we conceived our first daughter through plain old vanilla sex. Go figure.

Pregnancy, however, was not the rosy and sweet time that I'd hoped it would be. In fact, it was utterly miserable. I had hyperemesis gravidarum, which means I puked nonstop for most of the pregnancy. I actually lost fifteen pounds. I pushed my own IV pole around the Emergency Department while working as a resident admitting patients. I often had to explain to patients that my illness was not contagious! As if that was not bad enough, I was diagnosed with gestational diabetes around my twenty-sixth week of pregnancy. Miserable.

My second pregnancy two years later was equally devastating, and my gestational diabetes could no longer be managed with diet alone. I was on insulin five times a day by the end of the pregnancy. My dear friend and diabetologist, Dr. Edith Miller, told me not to have another pregnancy. If I did, it could either kill me or put me on insulin for the rest of my life. I decided to listen. Obviously, this body was not meant to carry children. Pregnancy was a beast!

Delivering them was a relative cakewalk.

So there we were in our late thirties with two beautiful biological children, but an overwhelming sense that our family was not finished. Adoption, we reasoned, could help us expand our family, and we were both wholeheartedly in favor of pursuing it. We had always had the thought that we would someday adopt a little girl from China or Korea. We knew we really did not want an infant, because neither of us relished that "blob" phase of a newborn, and were hoping to adopt a slightly older child. We went pretty far down the road with South Korea and Guatemala, as we had friends who had connections in those countries or had adopted from there previously. But six months into the process, an amendment to an international trade treaty tacked adoption regulations onto these countries. Instead of trying to manage the regulations, both countries chose to immediately shut their doors for international adoption.

Joe and I were very discouraged. But we did not give up.

We decided to pursue domestic adoption and explored adopting in our home county. We were not positive we wanted to be foster parents, as we did not know how that would affect our two young daughters. We thought that having kids in and out of our home through a revolving door could be very disruptive to their lives. We quickly learned that there was no appetite in our home county to place a nonwhite child in a white family, and the majority of children up for adoption in our county were not Caucasian. Evidently, we could not guarantee the appropriate cultural experience that the Department of Social Services thought such kids would need. Go figure.

We looked at private adoption in North Carolina. The laws

of our home state, however, are not particularly favorable to the adoptive family. We then started looking at adoption out of state, and learned that each of our fifty states has a different set of laws. The legal environment for adoption is a complete morass. Even with all our degrees—me as a doctor and my husband as an attorney—we could not navigate the process!

In utter exasperation one evening, we sat down and googled "adoption consultant." Guess what? There are actually companies in the United States that help with this process. For lack of a better analogy, they are headhunters. Basically, you pay them a flat fee and they maintain relationships with adoption agencies in states with favorable laws. So, instead of signing up with one agency and being at the mercy of whatever birth mothers walk in there, you are surfing multiple states and multiple agencies at the same time. Furthermore, the amazing staff at these consulting firms walk you through the whole process. It is like having a guide through the wilderness.

We found a firm in March, signed on with them in April, and on May 21, 2008, we found out about a birth mom in Tulsa, Oklahoma, expecting a Caucasian-Hispanic baby boy, due in July. We immediately overnighted our profile to that agency and waited. A month passed, and we heard nothing. We learned, however, that the lack of immediate response was not uncommon. Most women who come into these adoption agencies are in dire situations. They teeter between the decision to place their children for adoption or to parent the baby themselves. Every week we looked at a few more profiles and sent out a few more applications, but heard nothing back.

On June 20, we got a call indicating that the birth mom in

Tulsa was interested in us, but she was also interested in several other families. She wanted to talk with us by phone to help make her decision. The thought of talking to a birth mom on the phone was not appealing to me. I had no idea what to expect. What should we say? What questions should we expect from her? What was appropriate to ask or to share? This is where the consultant's input was invaluable. She got on the phone to help me with what to say and how to react. We had two calls with the birth mother over the next week, both of which were heart-wrenching. I was expecting to sell myself to this mother and prove to her we would be a good home for her child. But the exact opposite happened. She wanted us to know that she was a good person and making the right decision for her child. There was much weeping on both sides of the conversation. My heart broke for her in hearing about her desperate situation. She truly wanted to give this child more of a life than she could offer him. I was so impressed by her selfless love for a child.

At the end of the second call, the birth mother said she wanted us to have her son, and asked if we would take him. We, of course, said, "Yes!" I hung up the phone that night of June 26 absolutely elated! I called every family member and friend that I knew. We were going to have a baby boy in two weeks! Our dream of adoption was finally coming through. I know I did not sleep that entire night as I pondered holding my son in my arms.

But the very next morning, the consultant called us and emphatically insisted that we pull the plug on this opportunity and not move forward with this adoption. She explained that there were too many red flags with the birth mother. Unbeknownst to us, she had been refusing to sign paperwork with her agency, failing to return their calls, and blowing off her case manager in Oklahoma. Our consultant was trying to protect us. We had a relationship with the consultant, the consultant had a relationship with the agency, and this birth mom was with the agency. Our consultant told us to walk away.

I was devastated. In my heart of hearts, that baby boy was mine.

I was so confused, frustrated, and angry. This birth mom had chosen us. But according to the consultant, she had evidently talked to other families and indicated she had chosen them as well. *How in the world could this be happening?* I hung up the phone with the consultant and started crying. I think I pretty much cried all day Friday, all day Saturday, and into Sunday morning. But by the grace of God, I ended up in the prayer room at my church with two women who were also adoptive mothers. Although I do not remember their words, I know they prayed the sweetest prayers with me that morning, asking God to give me peace with whatever this woman decided. Perhaps I was going to push her to parent this baby, and that was the right choice for her and for that child. I didn't know why this was happening. I just knew it was not the adoption story I had planned.

By Sunday night, the weeping had stopped, and I was starting to feel numb. We were in our backyard on the trampoline with our two daughters, who were then aged five and two. For some reason, I had carried one of the house phones outside onto the deck. Around eight o'clock, the phone rang. It was our adoption consultant. I froze when I saw her number flash up on the screen. She never called at this late hour, so my heart jumped with hopeful anticipation. When I answered, she asked me to sit down. I could not breathe. I was sure she was calling to tell us the birth mother in Tulsa had changed her mind yet again. I was gasping for breath. She repeatedly told me to be quiet and sit down.

"I'm calling to tell you that I have B-O-G." I told her I was not following her. She said, "I have a Baby on the Ground."

"Well, did you drop it? What's the problem?" I asked.

She explained to me that she had just gotten a call from an agency in California that had a baby boy, mixed-race, with good APGAR scores, who had been abandoned at a hospital over the weekend. This agency needed a family in California tomorrow morning when he was to be discharged from the hospital. "If you say yes, he's yours, but you have ten minutes to make a decision, and I need you to put Oklahoma out of your head."

I was speechless. I asked her if we could have five minutes to pray. Joe and I then went to two separate rooms in our house and prayed like we have never prayed before. *Lord, there's a baby in California that needs a home.* My mom and dad were only an hour away and they could come to watch the girls. I knew we could probably make a red-eye leaving Charlotte that night. Yet three days before, we'd told a woman in Oklahoma we would take her child. Now, waiting for us in California, there was a baby that needed a home.

We met at the bar in our kitchen and circled it like we were playing a game of chicken. Joe wanted to know what God had told me first, and I wanted to know what God had told him first. We needed to have the same answer independently. Praise God, we both had an overwhelming sense of peace that we say yes. This baby needed a home and we could get there. We knew we had told the woman in Oklahoma yes to her child. We would never go back on our word to her, but we also believed deep down that we would never hear from her again.

We called the consultant back seven minutes later, and in that seven minutes another family had gotten ahead of us for this child. To this day, I am not sure about the details on how that happened. Evidently, there was another family who had just had a failed adoption with the same agency that had this baby. In the world of adoption etiquette, if you have a failed adoption, meaning you traveled for a child and the birth mom changed her mind, you have right of first refusal on the next baby who becomes available. This family just had traveled from Michigan to another state for a child, and the birth mother had changed her mind. Why we did not know this on the first call with our consultant, I'll never know.

Our consultant said that she just had a gut feeling about this. She felt like we needed to wait it out and see what this other family decided to do. I felt like I had been punched in the gut, twice. Within forty-eight hours, I'd had two babies dangled in front of me, only to have them snatched away minutes to hours later. This certainly was not part of my adoption plan! I started to think that we were completely wrong about pursuing adoption if our hearts and minds were going to be going through this horrific roller coaster of emotions time after time. I was not sure I could go through the torment.

I had no choice but to wait it out. *God, why did I have to relearn the whole "Your plan over mine" thing again?*

I'm not sure what was going through my head when we hung up the phone with our consultant that night. In fact, I felt we'd just put our lives on hold. We entered what I now call Adoption Purgatory. I called my parents and asked them to come to Charlotte to sit with my children. We put tickets on hold at an airline, and we waited. As much agony as we were feeling, I can only imagine how the other family felt. The agency was in Washington State, the baby was in California, the other family was in Michigan, and we were in North Carolina. Dealing with three times zone, four entities, and lots of emotional baggage was chaos. Add to that: I'm terrible at waiting. The next day was a Monday. I saw patients all day, and I'm thankful I didn't harm any patients with my head and my heart being pulled in so many different directions. Praise God for grace and mercy at times like that. We learned at some point during the day that the baby had been released from the hospital to a foster-care agency. I prayed that he was okay and someone was loving him well.

Around seven thirty on the night of June 30, I was sitting at the Charlotte Westin Hotel with all the partners in our large, multispecialty medical group. My jobshare partner was sitting at the table beside me. At some point during the meal, my cell phone rang. I fumbled to answer it as I ran out into the lobby. It was the consultant. The first words out of her mouth changed my life forever: "Well, do you have a name picked out? The other family has passed, and that baby is yours! You need to get on the next plane to California." I ran back into the meeting with a look of utter terror on my face. My amazing job share partner looked at me, took my hand, and said, "GO! I'll take care of your patients in the office. You need to go get your son!"

So we did. We got on the next flight to Los Angeles from

Charlotte. I don't remember much about the flight, but soon we were off the plane, had grabbed our rental car, and plugged an address into the GPS. We were basket cases! I do remember stopping at a restaurant to try to eat on the way, because we were a little earlier than our scheduled appointment. We went into a Target and bought some baby stuff as we had absolutely nothing with us—diapers, wipes, onesies. We had no idea what we were doing. We were in shock.

We arrived at the meeting place, a dumpy strip mall in a suburb of Pasadena, California, in a dated storefront with dingy stucco walls. Walking in, we saw a lady sitting at a desk, typing on a computer, holding a baby like a football under her arm. She looked up, smiled, and said, "Oh, you must be the Teagues." She got up from her desk, walked around and handed me the tiny bundle wrapped in a blue blanket.

"Well," she said, "here's your son, and, oh yeah, I stopped by Walmart to get you a few diapers, so here's a bag of them."

I collapsed onto the floor holding this little boy, as my legs could no longer support me. I unwrapped the blanket to see all of him and dissolved into tears. He was beautiful to me, but scrawny and pitiful by most standards. His legs were about the size of my thumb. His face was marked from what must have been a traumatic delivery. But he was the most perfect thing I'd ever seen. I was immediately in love. I'm not sure we ever knew his actual weight or length. It really did not matter to me. In my eyes, he was perfect.

When I was finally able to compose myself and we were leaving the foster-care agency, the lady behind the desk said, "Oh, by the way, I guess I need to see some ID before you leave." Talk about an odd transaction for the birth of your third child!

We drove away from the adoption agency, and within twenty minutes the phone rang. It was the owner of the adoption agency that had been handling this child. Mind you, this woman was in Washington and had never laid eyes on this baby. We had personally paid the foster care agency to "handle" him for the last twenty-four hours. Yet her words could not have been more cold or heartless: "You have your baby. I want my money. You need to wire it to me in the next twenty minutes, or I'm coming to get him." There was no "Congratulations on your new son" or "Thank you for moving forward with this adoption at a moment's notice." It was sheer, cold greed. We were seeing the underbelly of adoption, and it was not a pretty picture. Our first public outing with our new son was to a Bank of America branch in Pasadena, where we sought to wire her the ungodly amount of money she was demanding.

By the end of the day, we found ourselves sitting in a hotel room in Pasadena, California, looking at a baby with a penis. As parents of girls, we had absolutely no idea what to do with that! I am sure I was peed on ten times in the first twenty-four hours. We thumbed through the meager paperwork that accompanied him and pieced together his story. On the Friday night, June 27, as I had lain weeping in my bed in Charlotte, a thirty-seven-year-old birth mother had walked into a rural hospital in California farm country at 10:20 p.m. At 10:41 p.m., she'd given birth to a healthy baby boy. The nursing records indicated that she saw him for a period of less than five minutes. She then called the nursing staff and told them should could not keep the child. She wanted to place him for adoption.

The weekend social worker had come in Saturday morning, desperately trying to find an adoption agency. A Child's Dream was first on the alphabetical list and, thus, the one called. Although based in Washington, they had an office nearby in California. This birth mother completed a rudimentary intake form with minimal family history. For her own ethnicity, she listed "Prefer not to answer." For the birth father's ethnicity, she listed "Unknown." The name on the baby's hospital bracelet was different from the name on the adoption paperwork, and that was different from the birth mother's name. Before we had even gotten on a plane to travel, that birth mother had gone before a judge at the hospital and signed away her maternal rights. There was no one to ask about his history. He truly was an unknown child. We named him Titus Josiah Teague. Titus was the young Greek that Paul "adopted" as his son in the New Testament. Josiah was the one good king from the Old Testament. We figured he needed a strong name to grow into after such a rough start.

4

He Will Direct Your Paths

Trust in the Lord with all your heart
and lean not to your own understanding.
In all your ways acknowledge him,
and he will direct your paths.

Proverbs 3:5–6

I have to admit, these words out of Proverbs were not going through my head as we sat there staring at this helpless, wiggling little newborn blob on the bed of that hotel. Over those first few hours of trying to change a diaper of a baby with a part that squirted urine everywhere, we had the realization that four days earlier we had told another birth mother in Oklahoma that we would take another such "unwanted" child. We felt we owed that birth mother the courtesy of letting her know what had happened with our family. We called our consultant and asked her to get a message through the agency in Oklahoma to let that birth mom know that we had adopted. The question arose as to whether we would talk to her if she had any questions. We gave her permission to call us on our cell phones. We were in California, not North Carolina.

The next morning, July 2, 2008, I was sitting in this hotel room again, staring at this beautiful baby boy. My husband left the room to get some ice and, of course, my phone rang. It was the birth mother from Oklahoma. I'm sure my heart sank, as I had no idea what to expect from the conversation. I answered the phone and explained to her that our family was very different than it had been the previous Thursday when we had spoken. In a few short sentences, I told her what had happened in the last four days. There was a quiet pause. She then asked four questions, all four of which were about this baby we'd just adopted. Then she blew us away: "Well, that's great! Now my son can have two sisters, and a brother who's adopted just like him!"

I probably gasped, and I pray she didn't hear it. The next words out of my mouth would forever change our lives. "Sure he can!"

From that moment, she never wavered. However, she refused to go back to her adoption agency. She wanted us to adopt her child, but she did not want to do it via the agency through which we had found her. We never really knew why.

The next eleven days were a blur. I had to stay in California until all the paperwork cleared in both California and North Carolina. And of course, we nailed the Fourth of July holiday in two states that did not observe the same vacation days! So we had lots of time on our hands. Yet God showed up in so many ways to assure us we were on the right path.

The second day we had Titus, we went for a walk outside the hotel, looking to find a breakfast that did not involve making your own waffle in the hotel lobby. We stumbled upon a dive a few blocks from the hotel. To this day, I'm not sure what drew us in. We found ourselves sitting at a booth in a place that looked like it had not been updated in thirty years. As I looked around, I noticed pictures all over the walls of famous actors and actresses, posing in this dive with a quirky little Chinese gentleman. In every picture, the famous people looked like they were thrilled to be in the presence of the little man. In a few minutes, that same Asian gentleman popped out of the kitchen and came over to take our order. Immediately, he was interested in the squirming bundle nestled in the sling I was wearing. He insisted I get the baby out so he could take a look.

We ended up sharing our story with the engaging cook. He wanted to know everything: how we became interested in adoption, how we'd ended up in California, how we were exploring a second adoption. He was like a sponge taking in our information, dripping with grace and encouragement. Eventually, he took our order and disappeared back into the kitchen. He returned with our food and a tiny vial of oil. He asked if he could hold the baby. As we handed him over, this little man started praying over our son with fervor and faith like I had never heard. He anointed our son with blessings that I cannot even remember as the tears poured from my face; some were in Chinese, some in English, some in the language of the Spirit. I realized that the people in those pictures were "thrilled" because he had prayed over them as well. I can only imagine how many people this man had touched since he immigrated to this country years ago. He was small in stature, but his influence was enormous.

Eventually, as the paperwork process droned on, my mother flew out to Pasadena to accompany me, and Joe flew home to Charlotte to be with our girls. I did not want them to feel abandoned or alone while their parents left to get a new baby brother (or two). Daddy needed to be with his girls while I waited for the clearance to come home. I talked to the girls daily and let them "talk to" their new baby brother as well. I found myself nesting, even from California. I started trying to find an extra crib on Craigslist Charlotte, and sending neighbors and friends to go pick up odds and ends to care for a baby—or two. Did I mention we were not exactly prepared for this adoption? All our friends told us that adoption would take about eighteen months, but here we were at month three from the beginning of the process, and I was looking at getting not one baby, but maybe two!

God crossed our paths in California with a dear friend from our church in Charlotte who had moved there a few years back. She dropped everything to be my companion and tour guide. She prayed with me daily for the baby in my presence, and for the baby about to be born in Oklahoma, and for the two girls back home who were so confused as to what was happening. We passed the time touring art galleries, frequenting a Pinkberry yogurt shop, and strolling down Rodeo Drive, all with a ten-day-old infant in a sling! Titus was a dream baby. He rarely cried and slept most of the time I stayed in California.

We arrived back in North Carolina eleven days after we'd first met Titus. I will never forget the reception. Dear friends from church greeted us at the airport with huge signs welcoming our new son. People we had never met were in tears at the airport as they witnessed my girls meeting their baby brother for the first time. We drove from the airport to our home, and my small group Bible study was there with an ocean of blue blankets and clothes and supplies. I was absolutely overwhelmed. All my fears about not being prepared for this baby were calmed as I realized my church family had created and stocked an entire nursery for me. Our friends poured blessings over us in the way of prayers, presents, and the presence. It was staggering. I was elated to be reunited with my daughters and ecstatic to introduce them to their brother. Yet I was also agonizing over the fact that there was another baby that needed a home.

The next morning, I woke up to the realization that the baby in Oklahoma was scheduled to be born in six days and we still did not have any arrangements worked out with that birth mother. As I mentioned before, she did not want to go back to her agency, so we had no idea how we were going to work through this next adoption. We knew she had to find legal counsel or another agency as soon as possible. But she did not seem to have the initiative to make that happen, and we could not be the ones to make the first step. We again waited. And the more we talked to her, the less we thought that baby boy in Oklahoma would ever become part of our family. The mom was an emotional wreck, flighty and disorganized in every conversation we had.

That Friday, I received one of the strangest calls of my entire life on our home phone. An out-of-state number popped up on the caller ID. A man on the line identified himself as Mark, an attorney in Tulsa, Oklahoma. He said that a woman, very pregnant, had just walked into his office. He was convinced that she was going to give birth right there in his office. She had insisted there was a family at this number who wanted to adopt her child. He apologized for the inconvenience, as he said he thought she was crazy. But he was obligated to call the number and see if this was true, so he had stepped into the next room to call me. I chuckled as the baby on my own lap was wailing. I said, "I'm not sure who's crazier. Yes, it's true we are here, and we are in." He immediately confessed that he had never pulled off an adoption in three business days; this birth mother was scheduled to deliver by C-section the following Wednesday. He said, however, that if we were willing, he could do it.

I don't remember much about the flurry of emails, faxes, and legal paperwork that was exchanged over the next couple of days. I had a two-week-old, a two-year-old, and a five-year-old, and there was not a lot of rest going on in our house. At some point during these interactions, we made a decision to give this birth mother time to change her mind. Although we were invited to be there for the birth, we opted to wait and go out to Oklahoma two days later. The attorney continued to reiterate to us her instability. He was not sure she was going to go through with the adoption. We prayed and determined that if she was going to change her mind, we wanted her to do that without the pressure of our presence. We knew from all our reading about adoption and our advice from various consultants (our consultant was out by this point, and we were on our own, because the birth mother had abandoned the agency that had a relationship with our consultant) that birth mothers often flip in their decisions once they see and hold their children.

Wednesday came, and we waited and prayed with eager antici-pation. Believe it or not, we received a text from the delivery room with a picture of this beautiful baby boy with wild hair sticking up all over his head: *Here's your son!*

We bought tickets to fly out to Tulsa on Friday. This time, however, I was not leaving my family. I had been away from the girls for eleven days, and their world was upside down. They already had a new baby brother, our house was a revolving door of people they did not know, and the undivided parental attention they were accustomed to had been severely interrupted. There was no way I was leaving them again. So we bought tickets for everyone to fly to Oklahoma. My mother accompanied us as well, because we knew we would need help with childcare as we went to meetings with the attorney and the birth mother, and for visitation at the hospital. From the time we boarded the plane, I was not sure this was actually going to happen. This birth mother was agonizing over her decision, and she was ultimately in control. We felt, however, that if we didn't go, we weren't giving her a choice. And we had given her our word before we even knew about Titus. So we were going to follow through on this opportunity.

When you book plane tickets three days before a flight, it's hard to find five seats together, so we were all over the plane. I'm sure we were that party in the airport that you see and think, "I hope I don't have to sit near them!" On the plane, people were not happy about sitting beside a two-year-old or a five-year-old seated without a guardian. Eventually, people shifted so that my husband was with the girls, but I was alone several rows ahead of them. People look at you a little strangely when you have an itty-bitty newborn in a sling across your chest. Admittedly, I probably looked pretty good for a woman who had "just given birth."

As the flight took off, the gentleman across the aisle made the comment that he had delivered thousands of babies in his lifetime. I learned that he was a physician and went on to have a lovely conversation throughout most of the flight. Of course, the story of why we were going to Tulsa came out, and the story of the little bundle in my sling as well. As we were touching down in Tulsa, the gentleman let me know that I would be in his thoughts and prayers. He also offered his card to me to let me know that if I had any problems in Tulsa, he would be more than happy to help. It turns out that I had been talking to Tom Coburn, the US senator from Oklahoma, the entire flight and had no idea. My husband later told me I was an idiot for not recognizing him; I'll blame it on sleep deprivation. As I deplaned, his card in my hand was a sweet affirmation that God was sovereign and watching over us the whole time.

We arrived in Tulsa the afternoon of Friday, July 18. We dropped my mother and the three children off at a hotel and went to the hospital. The visit was surreal. I felt like I was going to see a family member who just given birth, not going to meet my future son. It was nothing like I had imagined. We arrived to find the birth mother rooming in with this beautiful baby boy. All I could see when we entered the room was a head full of wild black hair sticking out from a blue blanket snuggled up to her. She was nursing. My heart sank, as I could not imagine how she was going to part with her baby. But despite what she was doing, her words pointed toward going through with this process. She introduced him with a name that started with T; she knew that all our other children had T names, and she'd picked one that would fit in. Yet, she insisted she know the name we had picked out. We told her Tyre Jedidiah, and she immediately called the nurse and asked for his bracelet to be changed. Lots of tears and lots of conversations ensued about how we would do this adoption, and what was coming next.

For those of you who don't know much about adoption, there really is no such thing as an open adoption in the world of adoption legality. Open adoption simply means that you maintain some semblance of contact with the birth mother. Legal parental rights are relinquished at the time of adoption. Thus, we had to have a hard conversation with her about what she wanted. We made notes, and we knew we had to have specifics. We challenged her to let us know what she wanted going forward. She asked for simple things that were not threatening to me: she wanted pictures once a month for the first year; she wanted to call us once a month for the first three months; and she wanted to see him twice: on his baptism, and on his first birthday. After that, she did not want to see him, because she did not want to confuse him. After one year of age, she thought he would have memories. I don't know why or how I came to peace with these requests, but I did. They seemed to make sense.

Her other request that night was that she wanted to meet our entire family. It was important for her to meet the girls and the son we had just adopted. We agreed to bring everyone back to the hospital Saturday morning. Our biggest concern was what to tell our five-year-old daughter. How do we explain to her who this woman is and how she's related to this baby, who is supposedly coming home with us? We settled on explaining to her that the birth mother was his "godmother." God did use her to birth this child. I, however, wanted to be his mother more than anything in the world.

The next day was crazy. We walked into the hospital room. Immediately the birth mother handed Tyre to my husband, took Titus from my arms, and took my five-year-old daughter's hand and walked to the corner of the room. She stooped to talk to my daughter as they both looked over Titus. They had a conversation that I will likely never know the content of. The next hour we spent in that hospital room was a blur. Babies were handed back and forth. A toddler crawled on and off the bed. A five-year-old insisted on holding both babies. Everyone, including both babies, cried. I do have a picture from that visit that shows me sitting in a hospital recliner holding my four children for the first time. It is my absolute favorite picture ever.

As we walked out of the hospital Saturday morning, my five-year-old daughter took me by the hand and said, "Mommy, that lady is not Tyre's godmother. That baby grew in her belly. But that's okay. He's my baby brother, and he's going home with us on Monday." Oh, the faith of children!

We left the hospital, and the plan was to come back at noon on Sunday. The attorney was going to meet us there, and we would sign paperwork and then we would leave with Tyre, as he could be discharged that day. The birth mother was scheduled to stay an extra night and be discharged on Monday. Sunday morning, however, plans changed. The attorney called us to let us know that she had checked herself out of the hospital AMA (against medical advice) and she was taking Tyre home. She told the attorney that she simply needed a night at home with him. My heart sank. *It's over. We have come so far in seeing this beautiful child, and yet we are going to walk away without him.*

The attorney didn't know what to say. He suggested we go to

the hotel and wait. We sat at the hotel Sunday evening at a loss for words. My daughter once again crawled into my lap and held me close. She told me not to worry. "Mommy, it's okay. My baby brother is going home with us tomorrow." I held her. How was I going to explain to her that the beautiful baby she had held at the hospital might not be going home with us? We prayed, we asked for God's will to be done, and we waited.

The new plan was that we would meet the birth mother at the attorney's office at one o'clock on Monday. I started to prepare myself that she would not come and that we would fly home the next day, the same family who arrived in Tulsa on Friday. As we drove into downtown Tulsa on the morning of July 21, the wind was blowing, and it was 107 degrees. We snaked in and out of one-way streets, scrambling to look for a parking place. Then I saw the birth mother. She was walking down the street, holding Tyre with the blue blanket blowing behind her in the wind. I could see the tears streaming down her face. At that moment, I knew she was going to let him go. At that moment, in my heart of hearts, Tyre became my son forever.

We parked the car on the street and left my mother to attend to three tired, grumpy, and squirming children. Joe and I took the elevator to the twenty-seventh floor of the nondescript office building. We walked in, and very professionally yet casually, the attorney took the baby from the birth mother's arms, handed him to Joe, and asked us to leave the office. He said he would meet us back there at two o'clock. He and the birth mother had an appointment to see the judge. We turned and walked away. In silence, we went back to the elevator, down to the car, and drove out of downtown. I'm not sure we were even breathing at this point. We found the first place to pull off the road, which happened to be an Applebee's. We rolled out of the car, and my husband immediately turned to the bushes and puked. In twenty-three years of marriage, I've seen the man vomit only one other time. I think the reality had hit him: *What have we done?! We have four children!*

At two o'clock, we had a very uneventful signing of the adoption papers for Tyre to become our son. This time, we took everyone into the office—the two infants, the two-year-old, the five-year-old, and my mother. This attorney may be one of the most compassionate men I've ever met in my life. He reminded us that the law said we probably needed to stay in Oklahoma until the paperwork cleared. However, he looked around and said, "This family needs you. All I have for you is a contact number. I really do not know where it will ring. You need to go home with your family." We hurried out of the attorney's office and went to the airport to catch a five-thirty flight back to Charlotte. On the way, my five-year-old looked up at me and said, "See Mommy, I told you this was my baby brother and he was going home with us today!"

How could a five-year-old have such faith? She trusted Tyre would come home with us. She did not try to understand it. Oh me of little faith!

5

Children Are a Gift from the Lord

Children are a gift from the Lord; they are a reward from him.

Psalm 127:3 (New Living Translation)

Train up a child in the way he should go;
even when he is old he will not depart from it.

Proverbs 22:6 (King James Version)

Coming to parenting was a lot like coming to medicine. I'd really never thought of myself as a parent. The idea petrified me. And now that I am a parent, I know the fear was with good reason. In fact, my husband said to me after we had children that he'd never thought of me as the nurturing type. He even wondered what I would be like as a mother! Not sure that is very reassuring. But I suppose when you have your first child, some genetic switch flips inside you, and that mothering instinct just kicks in.

I mentioned before that I was all about planning the timing of having our children. God broke me of that need to plan when we struggled with infertility. He then quickly broke me of my desire to be in control with the birth of my first child. Proverbs 22:15 tells us that "folly is bound up in the heart of a child," but folly also lives and breeds in the heart of a parent!

Being a doctor is really just my day job. First and foremost, I'm a mother. And I guess I came to that reality kicking and screaming as well. That whole verse about man planning all things but the Lord's will be done? I have had to learn that all over again (and again and again) as a parent. Trying to balance the roles of mother and doctor is a juggling act worthy of the circus. As a parent, you'd better be ready to laugh.

The transition from zero to one child was certainly difficult, especially after eleven years as a married couple with no children. Joe and I were quite accustomed to doing what we wanted, when we wanted to do it, without having to think about another human's needs. Our first child, Trilla Belle, was born while I was in residency. Ironically, she surprised us after a year of infertility and a month of not trying. Although the pregnancy was miserable, her first year was a breeze for me. Joe carried the caretaking burden as I went back to work when she was six weeks old, on call every fourth night, working up to thirty-hour shifts. Joe came to the hospital when I was on call, bringing the baby for me to kiss and homemade hot chocolate chip cookies to exchange for breast milk! Good times. We jokingly say that he had the postpartum depression. Although we were both sleep-deprived, Joe carried the burden of the first infant because I was buried in my residency training. But by all standards, our firstborn was an easy baby. She slept through the night by about six weeks and was easy to get on a schedule.

When our second baby, Tattie Anne, came along, we realized we had gone from simple handoff to man-to-man defense. There was no break. When child number one goes down for a nap, you and hubby used to get a break. With two, when child number two goes down for a nap, child number one wants your undivided attention.

After an easy first child, I was expecting a similar experience with my second little girl. I was in for a rude awakening. At twenty-one days old, my second-born child was diagnosed with viral meningitis. A fever of 104 degrees is petrifying to any mother, but worse to a doctor mom who knows just enough to think the worst. Ironically, it was the first time in her three weeks of life that she was not crying. She survived a several-day stay in the ICU, but came home with an inconsolable disposition. She was labeled a colicky baby.

For the next three months, Tattie did not stop crying. I'm convinced that the meningitis somehow upset her nervous system, and she simply could not calm herself down. I tried every swaddle, bouncy seat, baby-on-the-dryer trick I could find. We finally realized there was nothing for us to do but wait until she could outgrow it. So she cried . . . incessantly! At one point during this period, our two-and-a-half-year-old, Trilla, slipped to the end of her rope. We were driving back from our parents' home, an hour-long drive, and Trilla spontaneously screamed at the blob in the car seat beside her, "Make the baby stop crying!" Can you blame her? It's what we were all thinking. My youngest daughter eventually outgrew the wailing phase, but her feisty spirit has endured.

The transition from two to three and then four kids in a

two-week period ended up being quite an adjustment for us and our girls. I heard a famous comedian once describe having a fourth child as like being in a pool, drowning, and someone handing you a baby! That is fairly accurate. However, in hindsight, I honestly think getting two babies at once was at least easier on the girls. They each thought they got their own baby brother. You could often hear them negotiating early in the day. "Sissy, can we switch babies today? Mine is fussy, and I like yours better."

Over the next year to eighteen months after the boys came home, Trilla and Tattie fell into unique roles with their brothers. Trilla, being the oldest, became the mother hen. Tatttie became the instigator. More than anyone, she had been dethroned as the baby and shoved into the middle-child role. I remember fondly a road trip wherein both boys, about eighteen months old at the time, were having a difficult time being buckled in their car seats. Tattie was tired of their wailing and had begun to taunt them from the third row of my Suburban. The drama escalated, and at some point she chucked her sippy cup at her brothers and nailed one of them in the head. I could see the knot forming immediately in my rearview mirror. From the driver's seat, I started my best parenting speech about how she should love her brothers and that was not an appropriate way to manage their crying. She called my bluff. She announced that she was getting out of her car seat, she was getting out of this car, and she was going to find another woman to drive her to her house. She was done with me and with this family.

It's always great to be considered just "another woman" by your child!

By my second Mother's Day with four kids, I was feeling out of control. I was trying to at least take care of myself physically. I had just finished a sprint triathlon (1000-meter swim, 20K bike ride, 5K run) the day before. My good-health advice to my patients can be boiled down to four words: "Eat less, move more." But there's no integrity in telling a patient to do something that you are not willing to do yourself. So partially to maintain my sanity and partially to be a good example, I had trained for this triathlon. And my whole family had come to town to support me.

After the race, we gathered at a restaurant for Mother's Day brunch. Of course, we had failed to make reservations, so we put our names on the list and decided to wait outside for a table to open. It was a torturous twenty-minute wait, juggling two boys in car seats and hungry six- and three-year-olds! The hostess finally called our names to sit down. At that moment, Tattie said to me she had to go to the bathroom. Why the urge could not have hit during our twenty-minute wait, I have no idea! I hurried her to the closest bathroom, a single stall that opened directly into the restaurant, and encouraged her to do her business. Once on the potty, she announced to me that she had to go number two. However, she did not like an audience, so she asked me to turn around and not watch. With my back to her, I tried to wait. Have I mentioned, however, that patience is not one of my virtues?

We weren't the only ones who needed the bathroom in this packed restaurant on Mother's Day. At least four times there were knocks on the bathroom door. Each time, I said, "Just a minute more!" Finally, exasperated, I whirled around to Tattie and demanded that she please hurry up. With her little legs dangling and her hand on her hips, she yelled back at me, "Mama, I cannot go any faster! My poop does not have a remote control!"

A few minutes later she told me she was done. We wiped up, washed our hands, and headed out to find the rest of our party in the restaurant. As I walked out of the bathroom, we were met with hysterical laughter. I realized the entire restaurant had heard her yelling!

Cheers to remote controls! *Ugh.*

> *Then our mouth was filled with laughter,*
> *and our tongue with shouts of joy; then they said among the*
> *nations, "The Lord has done great things for them."*
>
> Psalm 126:2 (English Standard Version)

At moments like these, you just have to laugh. Everyone else was laughing at us. We might as well laugh too. I guess this incident made me realize that we were raising a generation of kids who had no ability to delay gratification. Favorite shows on Disney are recorded so they can fast-forward through the advertisements. Who knew you would think you could fast-forward your bodily functions!

———

Having had two girls first, I was not prepared for the Y chromosome factor—or, as we jokingly call it in our house, "the penis factor." When one of the boys walks into the room and hits his brother upside the head for no apparent reason, we see the penis factor in action. When you ask him why he did that, he looks at you with a blank stare and says, "I don't know." Sadly, he doesn't. The penis factor is what happens when the frontal lobe does not engage before behavior. This is not a technical term, and you will not find it described in scholarly texts. It is simply our family-grown term for what happened when kids with penises entered our world. Life has not been the same. If I'd had the foresight to hire a reality-show crew to follow us around for the last eight years, we would be rich. Duck Dynasty would have nothing on us.

Toddler boys are tough. I'm not sure if it was because they are boys or because there were two of them. But their propensity for mischief was astronomical. On a rare day when I was home with all four of my kids in the summer, at one point I tried to unload the dishwasher. They were all running around like banshees, in and out the kitchen door as I stood there frantically stacking plates. I suggested that they find something to do together. Just a few moments later, I looked into the den to see Trilla and Tattie curled up on the couch as Trilla was reading her little sister a book. I had this moment of pure mommy bliss. How precious! I stood there relishing the moment for a good two to three minutes.

I stepped back into the kitchen and looked out the window, only to have my illusion of great motherhood shattered. There, on the deck, I saw the boys. One was eating dog food out of the dog bowl, and the other was draining the dregs of a Miller Lite out of the recycle bin! All I could think of was acute liver failure, and I ran frantically outside to take away his new beverage. The irony is that Joe and I do not even drink beer. Friends had come over the weekend before and deposited their unfinished leftovers in the recycle bin. Yep, real life is better than TV.

One day when I was trying to see a fully booked morning of patients, I got a call from the girls' elementary school. Although I never answer my cell phone at work, because it was the school's number on my cell, I thought I should. The secretary asked if I could come get Trilla (about seven years old at the time), because she had hurt her arm on the playground. Of course, the school nurse was not there that day, so no one could adequately assess her condition. The secretary had no choice but to put Trilla on the phone. She was sobbing. I tried to calm her down. I asked if she could pull herself together and ride the bus home in just two hours. Of course, she said no. I called my husband, who had a client meeting. I told him one client versus three waiting patients made him "It." He went to get her. Thirty minutes later, I got a call that they were on their way from urgent care to an orthopedist. She had broken both bones in her arm! Mom of the Year award for me.

Less than one minute after that call, I received a series of texts on my phone from the nanny, who was home with the boys:

Titus and Tyre on trampoline wrestling.

(No surprise there—they do that all the time.)

Titus pinned Tyre.

(Again, no big deal. Titus was twice the size of Tyre at that point, and he pinned his brother all the time.)

Was on my way to intervene when Tyre starts yelling:

My willy's gone! My willy's gone.

Titus bite it off!

My first thought was *Oh no!!!! I'm going to be on the front page of the paper. Local doctor makes two trips to urgent care—one child with broken arm and another with masticated penis!* As I'm thinking through these consequences I got the next text:

It's still there, but there are teeth marks on it.

Needless to say, I've made sure the big brother has not pinned the little brother since then!

So this is what I do: I try to manage life-and-death situations with patients while simultaneously trying to contain a household of mayhem. Some days, that works well. Other days, it just falls apart. Not long ago, I was frantically moving from exam room to exam room to see patient after patient, when my PA knocked on a door to let me know that my cell phone was buzzing incessantly. As I said, I try to ignore the phone when seeing patients, but my PA noted that it was my daughter who kept calling. I finished up with the patient I was seeing and ran into my office to check the phone. I wondered why in the world she would be calling me at work. I knew that the nanny was taking them to an outdoor play land with a NASCAR theme at Concord Mills Mall that day. I hit redial and my daughter quickly answered.

"Mom, Mom, did you see the texts?"

"No, I didn't see the texts, I am seeing patients!"

"Mom, Mom, look at the pictures. Tell me if Tyre needs stitches?!"

Oh, dear. I pulled the phone away from my ear to check my texts. Sure enough, there in my inbox is a series of pictures of Tyre's forehead with a gaping hole. Nice. Yep. He needed stitches. This was, by the way, not the first time. He already had a one-and-a-half-inch scar across the center of his forehead from running into the tailgate on Daddy's truck a few years ago. And he'd had stitches in his hand from picking up glass. (Remember that penis factor? It goes something like this: Don't think—just grab something sharp!)

I looked at my schedule and realized I still had fifteen more patients to see. Once again, Daddy was "It." The nanny drove Tyre to Joe's office, and they headed off to the urgent care. Again. Luckily, we have a children's urgent care fairly close to our house.

In the first seven months it was open, I was there six times. They jokingly offered me my own parking space! Once again, they put my kid back together that day. You have to laugh.

Even when I am not seeing patients, doing normal "mommy" things does not necessarily go like I think it should. You would think, for example, that going to the pediatrician would be an uneventful task for a doctor mom. When the boys were six, I took them in for their well-child check. Like any working mom, I was running late and trying to get them back to the nanny before I had to get back to work. I stopped at Panera to buy their glorious mac and cheese. As I was placing the order with the cashier, she leaned over and said: "Oh your grandsons are so adorable!" Ouch. Feeling the need to explain myself, I stammered something along the lines of, "Well, actually, they are my sons, and I was a little older when I adopted them." Instead of being happy with that answer, the cashier leaned back away from the register, cocked her head and looked at me, and asked: "So, do you want to adopt me?" The thought running through my head was not a godly one. I think it was something like: *BLANK no, but I want to teach you some manners!* As I jumped back in the car to drop the kids with the nanny, I immediately called my hairstylist and told her that, although we had been coloring my hair every eight weeks, we needed to move to every six, and could she get me in tomorrow?

I went on to my meeting, a late one, and got home about eight o'clock that night. At the age of almost six, my boys were perfectly capable of bathing themselves. But I don't trust them to run a tub full of water without flooding two floors of the house. So I asked my eleven-year-old if she would simply run their bathwater. They all trekked upstairs, and about three minutes later I hear screaming and yelling on the part of my ten-year-old. "Oh, my gosh, Mom, get up here now! Mom, I need help! Mom, I can't do this!"

How can running a tub of water be this difficult? Then I heard the pitter-patter of little feet running down the stairs. Our pediatrician always gives creative toys to children for their well-child checks, and my boys had been given Wikki Stix. Wikki Stix are bendable pieces of wax and string that can be molded into stick figures and various sculptures. As my boys ran down the stairs buck naked, I quickly realized the cause of the commotion. My precious six-year-old stood there with Wikki Stix creatively adorning his penis, not unlike a Christmas ornament. I looked at the penis, with the lovely decoration, and surmised there was no vascular compromise. Thus, I decided he could go ahead and take his bath with his junk so decorated. My daughter, who was still wailing that she was not going to deal "with that," was told she was relieved of her bathing duties. To this day, I have no idea how long the decoration stayed there, but I can assure you I will not be taking Wikki Stix as the pediatrician's gift again.

—◦─◦—

I can also assure you that I will not be opening up a Pandora's box with letters to Santa again this year. You know you're in trouble as a parent when your eight-year-old daughter completely outsmarts you—and Santa Claus, for that matter.

It was about two weeks before Christmas, and I had been

working diligently to keep Amazon busy with orders for specific presents for each of our children. We realized, as an afterthought, that we had failed to have the children write their letters to Santa. So we sat all the kids down on a Sunday afternoon to write their letters. Because the boys were not yet fluent in writing, we asked the girls to help their brothers. They carefully placed their letters in envelopes, and Dad was going to take them to work and mail them first thing in the morning.

About thirty minutes after Joe had arrived at work on Monday morning, I got the call. "Honey, we have a problem." Joe had opened the letters to Santa and realized that our eight-year-old's was stuffed completely full of cash. The letter read something along these lines:

Dear Santa,
All I want for Christmas my parents say that I cannot have, because it is too much trouble, it costs too much, and they will not pay for the food to feed it. So, here is a little cash to help you out.
All I want for Christmas is a guinea pig.
By the way, I will leave you extra milk and cookies as I'm sure you can work something out with my parents.
With love,
Tattie

For six months, Tattie had been asking for the guinea pig. Consistently, her father and I had declined the request, saying we did not want a rodent in the house and we did not feel she had displayed enough maturity to care for an animal on her own. We realized, however, that she had completely outsmarted us. The guinea pig was not on the shopping list from Amazon.

Do you have any idea how difficult it is to find a guinea pig ten days before Christmas in the largest city in North Carolina? I started calling pet stores. No less than ten calls later, I finally found a store with two guinea pigs left. I kid you not, the name of the store was The Last Place on Earth Pet Store. Two days later, I drove to the northern part of the city to procure the one present Tattie wanted from Santa. The darn creature spent the next ten days at my husband's law office. There was no way I was keeping it at my medical practice! OSHA would have had a heyday with that one.

On Christmas morning, our eight-year-old rounded the corner to see a guinea pig in a cage sitting in the middle of the den floor. For a good two to three minutes she squealed and jumped up and down with delight. Then suddenly she stopped, flipped around, and looked straight at me. "Mommy, are you mad at Santa?"

I paused, crinkled up my nose in disdain and retorted, "Yes, I'm very mad at Santa." For months, she would share her Christmas story with her friends, and tell them that her mom was so mad at Santa Claus!

Being the doctor and the mom just doesn't always go as planned. But the balancing act is full of joy. Have a kid . . . or four. The joy they bring is good medicine!

A joyful heart is good medicine,
but a broken spirit dries up the bones.

Proverbs 17:22 (New American Standard Bible)

6

I Can Do All Things . . . with Help

I can do all things through him who gives me strength.

Philippians 4:13

Of all the verses that were influential from my formative years, the first one I ever memorized was Philippians 4:13. I remember learning the verse, saying it in Sunday school class, and truly believing it with my whole heart. My parents instilled this verse in me as well. I never once remember my parents telling me that I couldn't do something. I don't mean that in the sense of discipline; I mean that in the sense of trying something new, whether it was a sport, a talent, or a hobby.

Once, I wanted to learn to ride a motorcycle or dirt bike, so my parents arranged for that opportunity. Early one Sunday morning, my dad pulled in the driveway with a mini dirt bike on the back of his truck. I was ecstatic! Immediately, I climbed on the bike and I distinctly I remember being told the location of the throttle and the clutch. However, I failed to grasp the concept of the brake. I sped around the outside of our house, ran into the vintage parked motorhome in the front yard, flipped the bike upside down, dumped all the gas out of the gas tank, pinned myself under it, and removed all the skin on my shins in a matter of thirty seconds! Of course, I tried this on a Sunday morning before church. The injuries did not, however, prevent me from having to put on my dress, my pantyhose, and shoes and head off to Sunday school. Despite the poor start, I was not allowed to give up my efforts. The next day, my dad took me to my grandmother's pasture and made me get back on that crazy dirt bike. Over the next few weeks, I mastered it. Then, like any typical teenager, I decided I didn't want to ride it any more. My father, in his infinite wisdom, had just borrowed the bike from a friend. Of course, I didn't know that until after I'd learned to ride it.

Such parental lessons about Biblical truths made indelible impressions on me. But as with many concepts from the Scriptures, sometimes we miss the intent, or we do not fully understand the message. It has taken me years to get the emphasis right on this particular verse. Even as a kid, I was drawn to the "I can" part of the verse. In my first two decades of life, I felt pretty invincible. For me, life had gone well. I thought *I could* do anything. Why? Because my own strength (wits, intelligence, resilience, whatever) had not failed. Over the last two decades, however, I have come to realize that what I can do or what I bring to the table does not really matter. It is the "through Christ" that carries the truth of the verse. No one has taught me more about that than my soul mate, Joe. But as with most other blessings in my life, I was not ready for him, either.

I made it through middle school and went into high school

carried by my own will and determination with an assurance that I was on the path God intended for my life. (I later realized I was dead wrong!) I was not the least bit interested in boys, because they would greatly interfere with my career aspirations. As typically happens, though, well-meaning friends tried to set me up. It was Christmas of my junior year, and both of my best friends had boyfriends. They were planning a Christmas party and invited me to come. I did not want to be the odd man out, so I declined the invitation. They insisted that they wanted me to meet one of their friends from middle school. I gathered he had gone to the same middle school as they had, but he was a year older than us. (This was a different end of the county, so our paths had never crossed.) They pointed him out to me at school, and I was a little concerned. He appeared to be something of an enigma. He was a jock, played baseball, and hung out with the athletes. However, he wore a lot of black, and a lot of Led Zeppelin T-shirts, and had a group of, shall we say, sketchy friends with Mohawk haircuts and gothic flair. I had no idea what to think of him!

I reluctantly agreed to the arrangement since it was a group setting and I would be shielded if I thought he was a total jerk. Joe came to the Christmas party, and we ended up having a great time. We just hit it off. We started dating over the next couple of months. Hanging out with Joe was easy. He was fun. He was kind. He was compassionate. He put me at ease with every interaction. He was real, and he drew out the real me. He was nothing like I'd anticipated from my first impressions.

On the night of his senior prom, however, he threw me a curveball.

We had returned to my parents' house and were standing in

the driveway, gazing at the stars, and he leaned over and said he thought he was in love with me. I then saw new stars (the kind that spin around your head when you have been hit with a brick) and freaked out. This was not part of my plan. I was in high school. I had no room in my plan for a longtime boyfriend or for falling in love. This is not what I wanted or I needed. Was he a great guy, yes? But I was not ready for this. So, as the clock struck midnight and he was walking me up my driveway to my house, I promptly dumped him. Yes, on his senior prom night.

I know you're all thinking: *What an evil witch!* But I was so scared. Scared of what Joe had said to me and scared of the emotions floating around inside me. I ran as far as I could in the other direction. Over the next few weeks, I found and solidified an opportunity to be a foreign exchange student in Paraguay for the summer with a group called American Field Service. A month after prom night, I found myself on a plane headed to Paraguay. I ran away.

I returned to the states for my senior year of high school, actually starting the year a few days late. I had not seen or heard from Joe in six months when I ran into his sister in the local mall in the fall. She said hello and indicated that Joe talked about me now and again. She suggested that I call him up. Talked about me . . . I'm sure he did! The things he would have to say about the girl who dumped him on his senior prom night were not likely too flattering. He was now a freshman at a nearby college and playing baseball for the school team.

Nonetheless, that conversation stuck in my mind, and a few weeks later I found myself with concert tickets to a band that we had enjoyed while we were dating. I decided to call him up to see if he might want to go. Surprisingly, he said yes, and the date was set. The car ride to the concert was pretty quiet. It seemed that we did not have a lot to say to each other. I was just hoping to get to the concert hall to have the music drown out the awkward silence. We arrived at the door to find out that they had oversold the tickets, the venue was at capacity, and the fire marshal would not let us in.

I was thinking, *Great, this date is already rather sour.* We ended up driving to one of my favorite spots at the lake where my family often camped; when Joe and I had dated, we'd spent countless hours there. Perhaps the familiar setting helped us to break the silence. Over the next few hours, we just sat and talked—about life, about classes, about how college was going for him, and about where I hoped to go. Again, that comfort and ease returned, and I felt in my conversation with him something that reflected part of me. I was at peace in his presence. At the end of the evening, we pulled back into in my driveway and he definitely got me back for the prom thing. He simply said: "I probably still love you, but I don't think I need you in my life anymore. Please get out of my truck."

Ouch. I walked into my house with tears streaming down my face. My mother and my little sister greeted me at the door. Their words of comfort were lovely. "We told you he was a nice guy; we're not sure why you ever broke up with him." Count on family to rub salt in the wound.

A few weeks later, Joe called. I don't remember the details of that conversation, but I do remember that we agreed that we should start over. Although we attended church and we'd talked about Christ during the time we dated before, Christ had not been at the center of our relationship. He suggested that we really seek

His will for what we wanted to do going forward. We agreed that a do-over would make a lot of sense. Within a few short weeks after that conversation, I remember thinking, *Wow, I am going to marry this man.*

Our dating life was somewhat unconventional. Joe was playing baseball in college. He rarely had a weekend free. I matriculated to UNC Chapel Hill and was on a scholarship, and part of the program included summer travel. Between my freshman and sophomore years, when I was working with the LAPD and Joe was doing an internship with Habitat for Humanity in Guatemala, our only communication for a thirteen-week period was a single telegram. Joe had no electricity, no running water, and no phone lines where he was. In the days before internet, email, or texting, a telegram was the best we could do.

When we did finally see each other at the end of the summer, he proposed, and I went back to school that fall with a diamond on my hand. All my friends said, "How impetuous!" They thought I had met someone over the summer and gotten engaged. They didn't realize that we had already been dating for years. They teased me about my "mystery boyfriend" who was never around.

Short of asking Jesus to enter my heart when I was six, saying yes to that proposal was the best decision I have ever made. Why would I say that? Well, I have learned more about how I need help through Joe than through any other person on the planet. When someone knows you better than you know yourself, he can look you straight in the face and tell you that are wrong or that you need to take a deep breath and relax. He has been the single most influential person in my life.

My parents love me unconditionally. But they did not choose

me. I was born into their home. Joe chose me. That's a different kind of love. It's one that accepts the flaws and foibles, not because it has to, but because it wants to. Love is not blind. It sees the mess. But loves anyway. I have experienced the depth and breadth of Christ's love for the church within the context of my marriage to Joe. "Husbands, love your wives, just as Christ loved the church and gave himself up for her." (Ephesians 5:25)

I like the term in Genesis about Eve being created as a "help mate" for Adam. I learned in Seminary that that term in Hebrew is a combination of two words, *ezer* and *k'enegdo*. The first means *to rescue, to save or to be strong, as in a savior.* Throughout the Old Testament, *ezer* refers to how God is an ezer to man. The other word, *k'enegdo*, appears only once in the Bible. From other Hebrew texts, it often means *against, in front of, or opposite.* The best definition I have heard is *exactly corresponding to or like looking at yourself in a mirror.* That's what I see when I look at Joe. I see the parts of me that I cannot even see in myself. He reflects God's love for me with flesh and bone.

And humor. He can tell me, with grace and compassion, what I need to hear without me getting crazy and defensive. Well, he would say that's true at least most of the time. He can tell me when the "I can" is out of control because he knows the truth is "I can't." And I can do the same for him. In case you haven't figured it out, I'm pretty strong-willed and verbal. He gets that and is not threatened by me at all. He makes me a better me.

Joe can often see me headed for failure long before I can. It happened when I was in seminary, blindly pursuing a PhD in psychology. When my supervising physician at my psychology internship told me that I was wasting my life and in the wrong field, it was Joe who recognized the truth in her statement to me. From that moment on, Joe never wavered in his belief that I was supposed to be a doctor, but it took me another few years to figure it out!

It happened again within three weeks of the boys coming home. Joe quickly realized we were in over our heads. We knew that having a newborn was difficult; our first child had been born when I was in the middle of residency. I had gone back to work when that baby was six weeks and one day old. Joe had stepped up to manage the sleepless nights then. We did it with our second baby, too, while also having a two-year-old in the house. We thought we could do it again. But two newborns plus a two-year-old and a five-year-old was overwhelming!

When the boys were three weeks old, I took a trip to water-ski camp with my girls that had been planned long before we even knew about the boys coming. I left Joe at home with two grand-mothers and a night service called Grandma's Porch that specialized in multiple babies. Two days into the camp, Joe called me and emphatically stated that we could not handle this ourselves.

I came home from camp at the end of the week, and Joe met me at the door with a stack of fifty au pair applications. He was convinced that the only way we could survive the next year or so was to have live-in help. I was horrified. There was NO WAY I wanted someone living in my house! My house was my kingdom. My domain. I sat down and wept. I could not even entertain the thought that I might need help. And I was embarrassed that I could not manage my own household. I was the chief operating officer. Was I getting a demotion? It felt like a hostile takeover. In my heart of hearts, however, I knew Joe was right. We had two crazy, demanding careers. We now had four kids with an age span of only five and a half years. That alone was nuts. God knew, however, something that I never knew. Sometimes, accepting help can be the most freeing experience in the world. And help comes in all forms.

As I cried and flipped through application after application, I was drawn to one of a young woman from Tennessee. There was a picture of her at her lake house with her family. The lake was and is such a place of calm and renewal to me. I knew that any girl who loved the lake would probably be okay in our family. We spent about two weeks talking to this girl, who had finished her freshman year at college but just felt directionless and wanted to spend some time being a nanny. She was hoping to go somewhere exotic, like Paris or New Zealand. We were looking for an international student. But our profiles just matched, and she said yes to coming to live with us. On Labor Day weekend 2008, Miss Jenny moved into our house.

Thus began our nanny chronicles. Looking back on it, I think we probably were crazy. Without ever seeing us face-to-face, her parents drove her from Tennessee to our doorstep and dropped her off. She came out of the car wearing her favorite black stretch pants and a sweatshirt, barefoot. She took my two-year-old daughter by the hand, walked around the house to our backyard, and crawled on the trampoline with her. I immediately knew we were going to be okay.

Over the next couple of years, Miss Jenny became part of our family. But the lines were blurred as to her exact role. The boys were six weeks old when Jenny walked in the door. For the first several years of their lives, Jenny spent more time with them than I did. They really could not tell the difference between me and Jenny as to who was their mother. The confusion started pretty soon after she arrived, and I didn't know how to respond the first few times. But eventually, I got used to the questions: "Oh, are these your grandkids?" "Is this your daughter?" Technically, Jenny could've been, if I'd gotten pregnant at eighteen, but I hadn't! I often was asked by friends on the outside looking in whether having a nanny bothered me. I had thought it would, but it didn't. I realized my children were amazingly blessed to have two women in their lives who adored them. They really did have a second mom.

If Miss Jenny's first job was to be my nanny, her second job was as a professional shopper. She took over the role of Teague household shopper—which had some great advantages! My children were dressed to the nines every time they stepped out the door, completely matching, coordinated, and adorable. Furthermore, they were known at every store in the mall and at the local Target. I remember clearly walking into Target on the weekend and the checkout staff greeting my kids by name and asking about Miss Jenny. They were shocked that these were actually my kids! Explaining "Yes, I am the mother" was hilarious!

I had always dressed the girls in matching outfits and made sure they were "put together" as well. Giving up that role was hard. But I had to accept that Miss Jenny did it better than I did. Again, relinquishing that "I can" role hurt. I had to accept the reality that Jenny had become a second mom and also the COO of the Teague household. It's amazing how giving up control can be so painful, yet so freeing. It allowed me the freedom to pursue my passions at work and church. Once I worked through the guilt of having someone in my house helping me manage it, I was relieved of the guilt of being caught at the office late. Because I knew that my children were being cared for and loved, I could pour my life into my patients and their needs.

Over the last six years, we have had four women in our home. As I write this, the fifth one is preparing to join us. After Miss Jenny, we had a series of international au pairs. These are usually young women (or men) working their way through university training who choose to spend a year or two abroad on a J-1 educational visa, providing childcare to a family. It is truly an awesome opportunity for the au pairs, as well as for the host families. That said, having someone living in your house is one thing, but having someone live in your house who doesn't share the culture is a totally new ball game. But for us, it has been an amazing blessing.

It's also a great source of stories! I was especially thrilled the day we got the call that the German au pair had gotten a speeding ticket going 83 in a 65. We quickly reminded her that Interstate 95 was not the Autobahn. At last count, the "Nanny-mobile" (a vintage Honda Pilot) has been wrecked seven times. Our ladies have failed to yield to a turning green, rolled through stop signs, backed over a mailbox, or just parked in the wrong place. (NO kids in the car with any incident, thank goodness, and no au pair hurt!) And every time we get a new au pair, it's like getting a new sixteen-year-old on our auto insurance. North Carolina doesn't care if they've driven in their home country for six years. When they get here, they're a new driver!

My kids can spin a globe and find places on the map that are the homelands of our au pairs that they might not otherwise have ever known. They sport soccer jerseys from Colombia and Brazil. Tyre has the fanciest foot moves on his soccer team thanks to the "coaching" of our current au pair. Tattie's favorite food is the Brazilian coxinha. (Look it up. BEST concept for a chicken potpie on the planet!) We now celebrate St. Nicholas Day (the German tradition of shoes on the doorstep on December 6 in hopes of goodies from the old man himself). The list goes on and on. My kids have been so blessed by the international influences of these amazing women in our home.

Embracing the *I can't do it all* has enriched the experience of my children and my home in ways that I could have never imagined. Allowing another human to mirror back to me my own failures, foibles, and flaws has blessed me in ways that cannot be explained. I am a hot mess. But God works through me when I get out of the way.

In the book of John, John the Baptist is asked if he is jealous that Jesus has come on the scene and is now baptizing people in the same way John has been. John replies: "'That joy is mine, and it is now complete. He must become greater; I must become less.'" (John 3:29–30) It has taken me over half of my life to realize this is the truth in Philippians 4:13. I really can't do anything. It is *through Christ* that all things are possible. And in that, my joy is complete as well!

7

Live Out Your Passion

We have different gifts, according to the grace given to each of us. If
your gift is prophesying, then prophesy in accordance
with your faith; if it is serving, then serve;
if it is teaching, then teach; if it is to encourage,
then give encouragement; if it is giving, then give generously;
if it is to lead, do it diligently;
if it is to show mercy, do it cheerfully.

Romans 12:6–8

When our second daughter, Tattie Anne, was in the fourth grade, she came home with a permission slip in her backpack for the all-county elementary school honors chorus. Her dad and I looked at each other in disbelief. *Honors chorus, really?*

Our joke in the house is that my girls received their father's tone-deaf gene, so when I looked at the piece of paper and at Tattie, I laughed. Tattie then explained that because she loves to sing, she wanted to do honors chorus. So, on the day of tryouts, she stepped to the front of the room, belted out "The Star-Spangled Banner" as loudly as she could, and the teacher liked it. She indeed had been chosen for honors chorus! Gotta love her chutzpah.

Tattie does love to sing, and has an amazing ability to memorize lyrics. It is rare to have a song come on the radio that she cannot quote verbatim. But yikes, I'd been telling her for years she could not sing, and now she had been chosen as one of the "best" singers in elementary school? I felt like the worst parent in the world.

Three months later, we found a permission slip for the Robotics Team. Unbeknownst to us, she had applied for the robotics team, written an essay (which we had never seen or proofed), and participated in a team competition to build a robot. And yes, she had been chosen as one of three kids in her grade to represent the school on the competitive robotics team. Again, she explained to us that she loved to build things and she knew she could help build the best robot ever. So she tried out for the team and made it. We had no idea that she even liked robots!

Tattie is a great example of someone who knows who she is and what her passions are. She does not need external approval. She follows her gut and finds her own glory. I pray she will always follow her heart.

As adults, we can sometimes lose that instinct to follow our gut. We seem to get lost in the mess of the mundane: paying bills, doing our jobs, commuting, falling asleep exhausted. I see it all the time in my patients. Losing who we really are, though, who we are created to be, can be soul-crushing and sanity-stealing. It can lead to both medical and spiritual crises.

I met Carrie for the first time a few months ago. She had first been seen at our Express Care walk-in clinic for a viral upper-respiratory infection. In reviewing the note from that visit, I saw that she'd recounted a stressful time at work and a desire to get out of her job. A week or two later, she'd had two back-to-back hospitalizations, wherein she'd been admitted to the ICU for severe dehydration and weakness. The hospital notes were vague; there was no discharge diagnosis to explain her constellation of symptoms. She saw me a few days after her last discharge. I entered the room to see a middle-aged woman, walking with a walker due to her weakness, accompanied by her mother. She was crying and visibly upset. I asked her to tell me her story.

Carrie was a very married, very successful banker with a young child at home. Over the last few months, her job had become more and more demanding and stressful, leading up to the recent hospitalizations. She recounted a litany of physiological complaints, none of which fit a pattern I could explain. She said her job was killing her and she needed to take some time away from it to figure out what was happening to her body. I agreed. We set out on a journey to find a diagnosis.

First, we explored what could be measured—some of the abnormalities of her labs. Initially, she appeared to be anemic. We thought this could be contributing to some of her weakness. We performed several studies to get to the bottom of this finding, and a simple over-the-counter iron supplement corrected the problem quickly. But Carrie's symptoms persisted. Next, we explored the causes for the dehydration and electrolyte abnormalities. Again, all tests were negative, and the lab abnormalities corrected themselves with the tincture of time. Finally, she was referred to neurology to see if she had a demyelinating illness (such as multiple sclerosis) that could account for her weakness. Several CT and MRI scans later, I received a call from the neurologist stating that her scans were normal, and that her pattern of weakness did not fit a diagnostic pattern. The neurologist was convinced she had conversion disorder.

According to the Mayo Clinic website,

> Conversion disorder, also called functional neurological symptom disorder, is a condition in which you show psychological stress in physical ways. The condition was so named to describe a health problem that starts as a mental or emotional crisis—a scary or stressful incident of some kind—and converts to a physical problem.
>
> For example, in conversion disorder, your leg may become paralyzed after you fall from a horse, even though you weren't physically injured. Conversion disorder signs and symptoms appear with no underlying physical cause, and you can't control them.

Indeed, this patient's weakness and symptoms were real. She was weak. She could not walk without a walker. However, she could not control the symptoms, despite finding no physiological explanation for them.

So, what was the cure? She needed a new job. In fact, if I had the prescription for "find a new job," I would be famous. I would be the next Dr. Oz! I cannot tell you how many times I have said to patients that the cure for their illness is a new job, a new outlet, a new passion, or a combination of all three. I practice in a city environment inhabited with many professionals who are successful, but their jobs make them miserable: bankers, lawyers, analysts, and traders, among others. They trudge to work, day after day, with the feeling that their souls are being sucked away from them. They have worked for years to get to this position, this rank, this promotion. Yet they are not happy. They are not fulfilled. They are not using the gifts they have been given to be the people they were created to be.

Scientific studies support the notion that hating your job can ruin your health. Take, for example, eating habits. Multiple studies show that job stress impairs eating to satiety and promotes overeating.[1] Basically, if you come home from a long day of work exhausted and depressed, you are more likely to skip exercise and binge on comfort foods. Hating your job also lowers your immune system's ability to ward off infection and increases your risk of serious illnesses, such as cancers, heart disease, and type 2 diabetes. Dr. Ichiro Kawachi, the lead researcher on a study that assessed the impact of job stress on the health of more than twenty thousand nurses, stated about his research: "We already know that the health status of smokers and sedentary people deteriorate more quickly than non-smokers and exercisers. Our study shows that job strain among female nurses has a comparable effect."[2] I can assure you, it's not just nurses! So when patients come to me with their physical and mental symptoms, complaining about their work, I ask them: *What is your passion?* Then I challenge them to find it, even if that means finding a new job.

Psychological theories are chock-full of the importance of finding who you are. Abraham Maslow's hierarchy of human needs is crowned with the concept of "self-actualization." Self-actualization, according to Maslow, represents the growth of an individual toward fulfillment of the highest needs. In particular, this refers to finding the meaning of life in who you are and what you do. His "triangle" of human needs starts with physiological

---

1   Dorthe Overgaard, Finn Gyntelberg, and Berit L. Heitmann, "Psychological workload and body weight: is there an association? A review of the literature," *Occupational Medicine* 54, no. 1 (2004): 35–41.

2   "Job strain 'as bad as smoking,'" BBC News, May 25, 2000.

needs, such as food, sleep, and air. Then, we layer on safety, or the concept of personal security that comes from social and political stability. Belonging and love come next in the triangle, and are based on giving to others in close social relationships. Self-esteem follows, and it is based on self-respect and positive feelings that are derived from such relationships. Finally, the triangle is topped with "self-actualization." This occurs when one embraces one's creative self, fulfills one's potential and finds meaning in life.

Carl Rogers also created a theory implicating a "growth potential." In his theory, the aim was to congruently integrate the "real self" and the "ideal self." If the two merged, one could cultivate the "fully functioning person." Erik Erikson said the same thing in his theory of psychosocial dichotomies. Some of these dichotomies included "trust versus mistrust" and "autonomy versus shame and doubt." Erikson's final stage of development, that of "ego integrity versus despair," is only successful if one finds the meaning of life.

Well, duh.

The whole time I studied these theories in undergraduate studies and in seminary, I kept thinking: *Yes, but that's not the whole story!* The entire narrative of Scripture tells us that we were created for more. We were each endowed with gifts, talents, passions, and propensities that God gave us to be shared with the world.

Before I formed you in the womb, I knew you;
before you were born, I set you apart.

Jeremiah 1:5

But what were we set apart for? Good works. Not meaningless, mundane tasks.

For we are His workmanship, created in Christ Jesus
for good works, which God prepared beforehand,
that we should walk in them.

Ephesians 2:10 (English Standard Version)

We, as humans, are NOT all the same. We do not have the same gifts. We cannot look at what others have, or what traits are valued in others, and expect to have them for ourselves. If we do, we are doomed to despair and confusion.

But when they measure themselves by one another and compare
themselves with one another, they are without understanding.

2 Corinthians 10:12 (English Standard Version)

Each of you should use whatever gift you have received to serve
others, as faithful stewards of God's grace in its various forms.

1 Peter 4:10

I know this truth. I see it manifested in my patients. Yet I had forgotten it, even with my own family.

When my youngest, Tyre, was about five, he saw the show American Ninja Warrior for the first time. He was watching it with his dad. At some point in the show, he looked up at Joe, eyes filled with wonderment, and exclaimed, "Dad, I know what I'm supposed to be when I grow up!"

This should not have surprised us. This is the same child who, at nine months old, flipped himself out of his crib. Yes, *out* of his crib. We had to put a netting cage over the crib to keep him in it for the next few months. When he was three, I received a text picture from our nanny, with a desperate plea about how to handle a situation. Tyre had climbed our rope swing in the backyard and was approximately twenty-five feet above the ground. I suggested the nanny not panic and allow him to come down by himself. Eventually, he did.

Since his revelation, Tyre has taken this Ninja "calling" literally. Everywhere we go and everything we do seems to present him with an opportunity to live out his passion. One day, we were at my oldest daughter's middle school softball game. Halfway through the third inning, a fellow parent tapped me on the shoulder and suggested I look behind me. There, on top of the fifteen-foot chain-link fence, sat Tyre. He had scaled the wall with ease and was perched precariously atop the fence. The concerned parent wanted to know if he should go get him down. I declined the offer. I knew that if I yelled at him, he could likely fall. I decided that he would come down on his own, just like he had from the rope swing, and it would be best to ignore the situation. Sure enough, five minutes later, he appeared on the bleachers with blood dripping from one of his fingers. He had cut himself on the jagged chain link at the top. As the great doctor/parent that I am, I didn't even have a Band-Aid on me. So I applied some pressure on the wound and sent him back to playing in the dirt.

Not long ago, Tyre and his brother were invited to a birthday party at an indoor trampoline park called Defy Gravity. I dutifully signed the release forms and dropped the boys off at the party so I could pick up some much-needed items at the adjacent Target in peace.

An hour and a half later, I returned to the party. Immediately upon entering the building, I was greeted by the party staff asking if "that child" over there was mine. The birthday party host parents were right behind the staff, trying to get to me. Now, mind you, when you get the question, "Is that your child?" there is a certain clenching in the gut. I hesitantly replied that indeed, that was my son, whom I could see swinging by one arm from a rope suspended high above a pit of foam blocks. And then there was a gush of incredulity by all who had been watching him for the last ninety minutes. Although I did not know it at drop-off, this facility had an indoor American Ninja Warrior training course, complete with the many obstacles seen on the television show. Evidently, my son had "mastered" the course in a way that no one in the building had ever seen. They described him as a "little monkey."

Tyre has asked us daily to take him back to that facility and keep practicing. However, it's not close to home and getting him there requires a chunk of time (which we rarely have) and advance planning (which we do not do very well). So he has turned our house into a Ninja warrior course. Every doorway is a place to "wedge" his way up, and every lintel is an opportunity for a pull-up.

Thus, every door casing in my house now has sneaker prints and every door header has nasty fingerprints. (Did I mention that little boys are gross? They NEVER think to take off their shoes at the door, and they NEVER wash their hands, no matter what filth is on their appendages!)

So recently, when I was making my way through the house with a pack of bleaching wipes and a Magic Eraser desperately trying to clean the walls, I had a moment of utter frustration. Just as I completed one door casing, he ran into the house and started climbing it again with muddy feet. I snapped. I explained to him (with a great deal of animation), that our house is not an American Ninja course and that I was tired of cleaning the walls, floors, and door casings behind him all the time. With tears in his eyes, he looked up and me and said, "But, Mommy, this is just who I am."

Well, he's right. It is just who he is. Hopefully, he can find a job that allows him to express all of who he is and displays his amazing gifts of climbing and agility. In the meantime, we are finding him a gymnastics class to have a creative outlet for his monkey tendencies and to save my house from certain destruction. Having four kids in the house with different genetics, different temperaments, and different gifts makes it a challenge to find the right opportunities for the development of each one.

Tyre's brother, Titus, despite his scrawny beginnings, is now built like a Greek god. At six, he was already huge. He is in the 95th percentile for height and 85th for weight. (Compare that to Tyre, who is 5th–7th percentile across the board.) Titus has a six-pack and defined glutes. His head is like a block. He looks like he should be a football player and appears very intimidating, like Ferdinand the Bull. But, like with Ferdinand, looks can be deceiving. Titus is gentle, kind, and compassionate and wouldn't hurt a fly. He loves to draw and "smell the flowers." He does not like soccer because it requires him to run too much. He tolerates baseball because the running involved is minimal. Plus, his brute strength and eye-hand coordination allow him to drive a ball way into center field, and that makes him popular with his teammates. The only problem for him is that he has to run after hitting it. Turn on some music, however, and the boy is a smooth mover! Yes, he can dance. But we are not sure that is his passion. We are still trying to help him find it.

We recently introduced him to the piano. The pitiful sounds are killing us, one note at a time. But he seems to love it. I had a friend who told me that right after we adopted him, she had a vision of him sitting in room full of teenagers, strumming a guitar and leading worship for a youth group. Maybe that is his gift. I don't know yet. But I do know I want to help him find his passion and follow it with his whole heart, even if that means earplugs for the next ten years!

Joe and I went to a Billy Joel concert this weekend. I was blown away by how great he was. Our local paper said that he played the "concert of the year." Joel is in his late sixties. He played for a sold-out crowd at an arena that seats over twenty thousand people. He even joked that he was surprised at the size of the crowd, considering he had not had a hit in over twenty years! But he is an example of a man who has followed his passion. His songs are timeless. He sat at a piano for two and a half hours and played his heart out.

Maslow would say that Billy Joel is self-actualized. Erikson would say he's found his ego identity. And Rogers would say he is a fully functioning person.

I'm not sure what God will say to him. But it is obvious that Billy Joel knows the talents that the God of the universe bestowed upon him before the beginning of the world. And he has used it throughout his lifetime to make beautiful music for all the world to enjoy. He found his calling to be what he was created to be.

As a kid in preschool, I remember learning a song that has stayed in my heart for all these years. Its theology is sound, and its message still rings true:

You are a promise!
You are a possibility!
You are a promise with a capital P!
You are a great big bundle of potentiality!
And if you'll listen, you'll hear God's voice;
And if you're trying, he'll help you make the right choices.
You're a promise to be anything He wants you to be!

—The Gaither Vocal Band

I am a promise. My kids are a promise. My patient is a promise. What does this mean for my patient, Carrie? She is not living out of the gifts God has given her. She is not living up to her full potential. God has so much more for her. Her job is killing her.

My job brings me life. I love what I do. I get to be a promise keeper and passion promoter. And sometimes, I get to write about what I do as well. What a great gig!

8

Be Still and Know

Be still, and know that I am God.

Psalm 46:10 (King James Version)

I don't do "still" very well. In fact, I don't do still at all. I rarely watch TV, because I cannot be still that long. If I am sitting, something is always moving on my body. I jiggle my legs. And twiddle my fingers. I start to do one thing and then get up and start something else. I prefer to stand and type than sit and type so I can bounce up and down on my toes. My grandmother had a phrase for people like me: "a hot fart in a skillet."

Well, I suppose God's sense of humor has given me at least one child, Tyre, who fits this definition to a T. In fact, he asked for a FitBit—for his seventh birthday. No way I was going to spend that kind of money on a gadget he was sure to lose in a few weeks. Luckily, there is a kid version known as a KidFit. We placed the bright blue band on his arm out of curiosity for us, more than anything else. The second day he wore it, the download said he'd walked 13.5 miles! Yes, he moved the equivalent of a half marathon in just one day! I own a FitBit, but I refuse to wear it. I'm not sure

I really want to know how many miles I put on my chassis on a regular basis.

Despite this, "Be still, and know that I am God" resonates with me. I guess I am drawn to the concept because I struggle with the reality of stillness. Yet I desperately want to know God. I have wrestled to understand and implement this juxtaposition of two concepts my whole life. Since physical stillness does not work for me, I have tried to find ways to be spiritually, emotionally, and mentally still. Again, this is not easy, and ironically, some of my most spiritually stilling times are when I am exercising. If I am exercising, I am seeking God's conditioning of my soul.

For most of my adult life, physical exercise has been a huge part of my routine. Since becoming a physician, I've realized there is no integrity in telling a patient to do something that I am not willing to do myself. I have always enjoyed running. In fact, middle distance running was my sport in high school. Running is a time when I do my best praying. I'm sure that the folks in my neighborhood think I am schizophrenic, as I often pray out loud and mumble to myself and to God while I am running. *There goes that crazy lady talking to herself again.* Well, I'm not talking to myself. I am talking to my best friend.

In the last few years, however, I have branched out to new things. I get bored easily, so even my workout regimen needs to be mixed up. A trainer introduced me to the sprint triathlon, a race involving a swim of 750 meters, a bike ride of 20 kilometers, and a run of 5 kilometers. I completed a few of those, until I got bored with the training. The hardest of the events in a triathlon for me is biking. And due to my crazy schedule, I had to "train" in a spin class rather than on the open road. Did I mention that being still was torture for me? Spinning my legs in a circle and going nowhere was miserable.

In the last few years, I have gotten into CrossFit classes. The combination of strength training and aerobic spurts is invigorating. My attraction to CrossFit highlights two of my character flaws. First, as noted above, I get easily bored. CrossFit is a different workout every single day, and someone else tells me what to do and how to do it. I just show up. Second, I am fiercely competitive (in case you have not figured that out from my story so far). CrossFit is done in a class environment. And I am often one of the oldest people in my class. Doing a WOD (workout of the day) with people half my age pushes me to work harder than I would on my own!

The analogy of physical training helps me to understand and experience spiritual training. Sometimes, the pain of sore muscles and cramps in my calves reminds me of the practice I need to put forth to live in sync with God's plan for my life. When I was pregnant with my first child, Trilla Belle, and utterly miserable as I saw my body being invaded by an alien, my sweet husband came to me and offered a deal. He knew that I had always wanted to run a marathon, so he promised me that in the year after our daughter was born, we would train together to run one.

Well, three weeks before her first birthday, we ran the Disney Marathon! The whole goal of getting my body back did not work out so well. The fine print of what pregnancy does to one's body should be in bold at the top of the page! But I learned so much about training for something that I really wanted to do. As I extended my distance every single week during the training process, I found that the long runs became easier and easier. I was still sore, but the soreness did not last as long. I learned that I had to go for the training runs, even when it was cold, raining, or I just did not feel like it. Learning to know God is the same way. Often, I have to talk to God even when I don't feel like it. It's the only way I know Him more.

The marathon was on my bucket list, so I checked that off and have no desire to run another one. But I have run several halves since then. For running, you have to gradually increase distance up to an event to be prepared. You can, however, improve your stamina and your strength by doing other things. I think this works for our spiritual lives as well. Take, for example, prayer. There is no way to improve your prayer life other than praying. But sometimes you have to change your mode of communication. For instance, certain seasons in my life have lent themselves to journaling over a particular scripture. Other times have lent themselves to doing Bible studies with a group. Being around other people who are seeking God pushes me to try harder. (Just like being in my CrossFit classes.) Still other times I have focused on reading a contemplative book. Through all these times, exercising and talking with God have centered me.

The only other place that I am "still with God" is on the water. I love being on a lake. On water skis, to be exact—okay, that's not exactly a "still" activity. At an early age, I started to see the lake as a place of escape, restoration, and rejuvenation. My passion for water-skiing goes way back to my childhood. I have no memory of learning to ski. When I was born, my parents were in a water-ski club that consisted of twenty families. Each year, this club produced a water-ski show comparable to the ones performed at Cypress Gardens. My mother, being the theatrical one, produced the shows, complete with full costumes, choreography, narration, and music. My parents tell me I was eighteen months old when I learned how to ski. Again, I have no memory of learning. I just remember always loving it. By the time I was eleven, I was climbing to the top of the triple-decker pyramid. I also performed water ballet, slalom tricks, trick skiing, and barefooting. Every weekend of my childhood was spent camping on the hundred-acre tract of land that the ski club had leased from the local power company. I knew more about an inboard ski boat by age thirteen than most people know in their lifetimes!

Every year, we actually go to water-ski camp for a full week in the summer. For my daughters and me, this past summer was our tenth year in a row. For my husband and the boys, it was the sixth. My first trip to camp was a Christmas present from my sweet husband to me and our girls the Christmas we started the adoption process. He knew that water-skiing had been an important aspect of my childhood, and he thought it would be a great way for me to bond with the girls before a new addition came home. We'd anticipated that the *waiting* part of the adoption process would last awhile—little did we know we would already have two six-week-old infants by the time the trip rolled around. Because I was so in shock after the adoptions, and because my girls had very little mommy time that summer the boys came home, Joe insisted that I take that first trip with them. I had no idea that we were establishing a family tradition that would carry through to this day.

Believe it or not, the world's largest water-ski and wakeboarding school is in North Carolina, in Lillington. Don't try to look it up; it won't make the map, but for the sake of geography, it's about an hour south of Raleigh. The school was started by the twenty-six-time US National Champion April Coble Eller and is a great story of her family following their passion. When April was in college, she convinced her parents to purchase an abandoned mining site that was absolutely perfect for the creation of a ski school. Over the past twenty-five years, she and her family have created an amazing environment for kids and families to come and share the passion of water-skiing and wakeboarding. Because of her stature in the world of water-skiing, she recruits the best instructors from around the world.

My friends think we are absolutely nuts going to water-skiing camp. Joe and I both take a full week off work to go to the camp. We stay in hot, cramped cabins. We eat red rockets (also known as hot dogs) and camping food. We rise at the crack of dawn with all the kids and participate in all the activities. By the end of the week, Joe and I are so sore we cannot move. However, we know we have created amazing memories with our kids.

The week is also unplugged. Sure, we have some iPads and iPhones and the computer with us. But they rarely get touched because we are so busy having fun. This gives us a chance to mentally unplug. I often tell patients that I am not sure our brains have the capacity to process the amount of data thrown at us on any given day, which is way different from when I was growing up. I actually remember a time when you could only get three channels on the TV—ABC, NBC, and CBS if the rabbit ears were tweaked just the right way on the television. And, oh yeah, you had to get up off your butt to move the ears or change the channel. Now I have approximately three thousand channels to choose from at any given moment, and thousands of shows. By the time you surf all that, you've wasted an entire evening!

I actually remember getting my first cell phone. It was in a black bag the size of a carry-on suitcase and weighed about ten pounds. The battery was good for only about thirty minutes, so it was never turned on and only used for emergencies in the car. I even remember getting my first computer as a freshman in college. It too was massive and heavy, and lugging it up to the fourth floor of my un-air-conditioned dorm was an ordeal. Now, I have one, sometimes two, smart devices on me at all times. I can find the weather in Bangladesh with two swipes of a finger (if I need to, which I don't). I can easily receive twenty to thirty emails or texts an hour. And those never stop, even when I'm asleep. Every member of my family has a smart device. Any time I pick up one of them and open a browser, there are rolling advertisements of the last thing I searched for on any device! It's crazy.

So it's a relief that the time spent with our kids at water-ski camp isn't hampered by technology. It's about the simple things—learning to wait your turn, to be part of a larger group, and to do things you've never done before. It's about physically pushing yourself to do things you don't think you can do. It's about overcoming your fears and surviving. And it's about letting your kids see you try something and struggle.

That first year at the camp, I stepped off on a slalom start and popped my hamstring the very first day (this was likely attributable to the stress I was under). I came back to Joe and two newborns on crutches! But I keep going back. Each camp week, one camper is awarded the "Crash of the Week" award. This award is chosen by a vote of all the instructors and is bestowed upon the person who takes the most wicked fall—and gets back up and tries again. Two years ago, Joe was working hard on the slalom course and took an epic fall; he became the winner for our camp week! We had the

T-shirt framed, and it's displayed prominently on the wall of his law office. In big, fat letters it reads: *I survived the CRASH OF THE WEEK!*

Although we have taken a few knocks at camp, we have overcome our struggles and fears and accomplished amazing things. The girls were two and five the first year, and seeing them win the Itty-Bitty Skier award that year and for the next several was so life-giving. When Tyre (yes, our own American Ninja Warrior) was just five, he mastered slalom skiing. They said he was the youngest slalomer they had ever seen! That same year, at age forty-four, I ran the fastest slalom course I'd ever done. I didn't break any records, and I'll never enter any competitions for my performance, but it was awesome to share my personal best with my kids.

I love seeing my kids push themselves to meet goals they had never thought possible. When you arrive at camp, there is an orientation session where everyone is expected to stand up and share his or her name and goal for that week. My kids really agonize over choosing their goals for the week. Seeing them work through this process and pick goals that are challenging but meaningful has been enlightening.

But the real lessons of water-ski camp are found in the time we spend together as a family in an unrushed, unplugged, and unhurried week.

> He says, "Be still, and know that I am God;
> I will be exalted among the nations,
> I will be exalted in the earth."
>
> Psalm 46:10

Observing the Sabbath means that you should take the time to rest, step away from the chores of daily life, and do what brings you joy. The Old Testament talks a lot about holy days. We get our word holiday from holy days. As a Christian, I don't observe the seven feasts in the Old Testament as holy days (the current Jewish holidays), but I understand the concept of the Sabbath and taking time away. I've been able to teach my children this concept through stepping away from our routine and having time like water-ski camp. It is a time completely devoted to watching them and finding joy in their accomplishments and in their struggles. And where else, as an adult, do you go do something fun four nights in a row—like getting homemade ice cream, bowling with your kids, or playing on an outdoor water park until your arms hurt from climbing the inflatables?

I hope my kids remember these summer weeks. I hope they remember that on the banks of the lake I cheered them on, that I laughed with them and cried with them, and that I took a holiday with them. I hope they see how important it is to be still and know that He is God. Somehow, through this process of "exerting ourselves" and stepping away, I hope I am teaching them the concept of sometimes moving to be still. At the very least, I know this will work for Tyre, the hot fart in the skillet!

9

Let Your Light Shine

In the same way, let your light shine before others,
so that they may see your good works
and give glory to your Father who is in heaven.

Matthew 5:16 (English Standard Version)

I had lunch recently with a dear friend who is facing a huge career move. Although this change is not by her choice, she is totally and completely at peace with it. She has worked for her organization for seventeen years. She started as a front-line provider of health care and worked her way up to be a vice-president-level administrator. I have watched and admired her for years. She is gifted, talented, and profoundly outspoken when she sees things that need to be changed. She is a team builder and brings out the best in people. She says she's headed to Washington to change health care. I know her, and I believe she'll do it.

She told me about her recent experience of going through a year-long professional coaching process. Basically, the program entailed meeting with a small group of women near the same season in their careers, and evaluating where they were in their lives and where they wanted to be. I was intrigued. She shared with me two things that had really helped her walk through this season.

The first concept was one that I had heard before, but forgotten:

FAIL: First Attempt I Learned

I love it! It so rings true in my experience as a mother, a friend, a doctor, and an administrator.

Take, for example, my never-ending struggle with getting my kids to clean up their clutter. With three adults, four children, one dog, and two cats in our household, the clutter never ends. I am always tripping over something, tossing something up the stairs, or yelling at a kid to come get whatever toy, article of clothing, or food particle has been left in an inappropriate place. It's exhausting. I tried every technique from the Love and Logic parenting classes I've taken, but when those failed, I became known as the "yeller" in the house. (Note: not an approved Love and Logic tactic.)

A patient shared with me an idea that seemed novel, so I thought I'd try it out. I went and purchased a cheap plastic bin at Target. At the end of each day, I wander through the first floor of my house and pick up the socks, shoes, matchbox cars, marbles, and even iPads that are strewn all over and put them in the bin. I then place my bin in my closet for safekeeping. Inevitably, someone realizes that I have confiscated their favorite UGG or electronic gadget. My response is that the article is mine for the rest of the week. My offspring can "spring" their loot from the Mommy Bin with the appropriate bail. As the bondsman, I have decided the appropriate bail is usually a chore of the child's least liking. Cleaning a toilet or washing the dog are among my top ten. Now, I would be lying if I told you that I had a neat house. However, I can say that the clutter has greatly diminished. My toilets are a little cleaner as well! Indeed, I failed many times, but I learned, and I have found a system that works.

In the exam room, I am reminded of my failures as well. Just a few weeks back, I had a patient who came in with a family member truly angry and upset with me due to an interaction a week or so before. At the earlier encounter, the patient was reestablishing care. I had not seen him in over two years. At that visit, he recounted a complicated story to me concerning an injury for which he was receiving care from multiple different providers in multiple locations. I was asked to write him out of work for the treatment of this condition. I explained that he needed to find care in one location and that the doctor or doctors providing that care needed to provide a work excuse. Although I thought I had explained this well, I had not. The patient stated that I made him feel judged for going to multiple doctors. Furthermore, he had walked out of my office feeling worse than he walked in. Well, I failed to do no harm. I have cried with patients on multiple occasions, concerning a devastating diagnosis or a seemingly insurmountable social situation. This time, however, I cried because my heart hurt. I asked for the patient's forgiveness and I asked to pray with him.

A few weeks later, the patient came in a third time for a follow-up visit. He stated that he had never had a doctor pray with him before. Furthermore, he'd never had a doctor be so transparent with her "failure" of communication. He said he appreciated my candor and knew that I truly cared about more than just his pain. And I do care. Ironically, my failure had opened the door for a better patient relationship, one that I will continue to grow and nurture. Sometimes, it takes failure to provide focus.

This idea of failure and learning from failure is the premise of basic scientific theory. Medicine is full of these stories. In my relatively short career, I have experienced many of these failures (and surprises) related to medications. In residency, we had a fairly new antibiotic at our disposal. It was heralded as one of the best in its class and perfectly safe. I'm sure that I prescribed it dozens of times for very sick patients with serious infections in the hospital. Then in the middle of my residency, the FDA suddenly pulled the medication from the market. Apparently, it could cause severe liver failure. Such reactions were often fatal, and one such fatality actually occurred at our hospital. This supposedly fabulous antibiotic that had been deemed a lifesaver ended up being a life taker.

When I was studying the heart in medical school, the current wisdom was that you did not want to suppress the beta cells in the heart when someone had had a heart attack. Then, as I moved into residency, more data came out showing that the use of beta blockers in the acute setting of a heart attack saved lives. Go figure.

Take another example: the new generations of antidepressants that help restore the chemical balance in the brain and help to pull people out of their depression and anxiety. Abruptly in 2007, after I had been prescribing these medications liberally in practice for years, the FDA issued a black-box warning on these medications, as there was found to be an increase in suicides in the young men and women taking them. Apparently, the drugs treat the paralysis of depression before actually treating the depressed feelings. So depressed people had the "energy" to act on their feelings of hopelessness and futility. Sadly, I just experienced this with a distant relative. The family member started on one of these medications. His volition was "unstuck" but his feelings of desperation were still raging. He took his own life. It was devastating.

We loathe failure. We don't want to be wrong and admit it. Yet at the same time in medicine we don't want to admit we are right too quickly. The FDA so regulates medication in this country that on average it takes twelve years for a new medicine get to market here, longer than in any other Western country. We have amazing cures for diseases sitting in trials right now. We just don't want to make a mistake. People die because we're afraid to bring a new agent to market. We err on the side of safety, and we may fail on that front as well.

———

The second thing my friend shared with me from her coaching group was a quote from Marianne Williamson's *A Return to Love* that she had learned through her coaching program. It resonated with me and my musings on fear and the resulting failure to thrive in our souls.

> Our deepest fear is not that we are inadequate. Our deepest fear is that we are powerful beyond measure. It is our light, not our darkness, that most frightens us. We ask ourselves, "Who am I to be brilliant, gorgeous, talented, fabulous?" Actually, who are you not to be? You are a child of God. Your playing small does not serve the world. There is nothing enlightened about shrinking so that other people won't feel insecure around you. We are all meant to shine, as children do. We were born to make manifest the glory of God that is within us. It's not just in some of us; it's in everyone. And as we let our own light shine, we unconsciously give other people permission

to do the same. As we are liberated from our own fear, our presence automatically liberates others.

Two weeks later, I was attending a women's leadership breakfast, and the woman giving the invocation used this same quote, noting that it hung on a plaque beside the bed of both of her daughters. She read it to them on a regular basis, reminding them to be all that God intended them to be. The speaker for the meeting then picked up on this theme of how we tend to downplay our talents. (I was dumbfounded that the woman giving the invocation had no idea of the message the speaker would be delivering. Sometimes, at least in my life, coincidence is God's way of being anonymous.)

The speaker, Victoria Budson, was the Founding and Executive Director of the Women and Public Policy Program at the John F. Kennedy School of Government at Harvard University. I was intrigued by two concepts she presented. First, she said women (and by extrapolation, all children of God), need to develop the talent to toot their own horn without blowing it. She gave an example of which I am guilty all the time. When I have had the opportunity to work with my leadership team on an initiative, like meeting our quality metrics for 2015, I often responded to a compliment with the statement, "Oh, thank you so very much. But it was not me. It was all my team. I really did not do anything." When a woman says that, people around her tend to believe it. They assume she really did nothing and played no role in the success of the team. When a man says that, however, people around him assume he's just being modest and he really did make a significant contribution. Budson cited research that both men and women make that same attribution error. We are "primed" to expect men to be strong leaders and women to be self-effacing. You can put cucumber in the brine pretty easily, but it is hard to get the brine out of the cucumber!

The other concept Budson covered was the idea of problem solving and heterogeneous teams. In summary, homogeneous teams (all male, all female, all engineers, all Southern) tended to enjoy solving problems together and then feel really good about their outcomes (e.g. "We nailed it!"). High fives are given all around, even if the outcome is not objectively the best solution. Heterogeneous teams (mixed gender, race, ethnicity), in contrast, tended to solve much more complex problems with better objective solutions. Their subjective experience, however, was less satisfactory. They described the experience as challenging and unpleasant, and they were unsure whether the outcome was right. Furthermore, team members "held back" on contributing their full potential, especially women. Female engineers failed to contribute the full depth and breadth of their knowledge when in heterogeneous teams. They were afraid to "shine too brightly" or "to fail," so they didn't give their all.

We need to be all that we can be in order to bring out the best in others. As the Marianne Williamson quote notes, we need to shine to give others permission to shine.

Scott Carbonara, who is known as "the Leadership Therapist" and is a nationally recognized author, speaker, and educator on engaging employees, spoke at another event I attended on the idea of creating teams of people who make one another better. He suggested that you need to surround yourself with the right people.

They need to be different from you, but complementary to you. He suggested that our word for "tribe" comes from the Greek word *tribos*, which means "to rub." It refers to the rut or path formed by constantly rubbing against something. I did some research on the word myself, and it is plausible that the Greek word likely came from the Latin term *tribus*, meaning a group of people claiming common descent. I like the concept that people around you, even the hard ones, make an impression on you. That is clearly suggested in Scriptures, in Proverbs 27:17: "As iron sharpens iron, so one person sharpens another."

God gave me a concrete example of this when I had my Cutco knives sharpened in my home. I've had these knives for over twenty years. A friend introduced me to a college student working his way through college selling knives, and I felt obligated to let him stop by and give me a complimentary sharpening (and an obligatory sales pitch). Watching this young representative rub my knives against what looked like rough rocks was fascinating. It was a multistep process, involving several different textures of flint to get the knives back to their original condition. I thought about this process and how God may look at us like dull knives as well. We have to rub up against each other to restore and maintain sharpness. And if we fail to show our rough sides, others cannot be sharpened by our presence.

———

There is real irony here. Failure: we hide. Success: we hide. We don't want to be wrong, but we don't want to be too right either. We shrink away from shining too brightly so that we don't bring too much attention to ourselves. We humans are schizophrenic in our behavior. I've tried to make sense of this with the whole narrative of Scripture. I think God wants to use all of us, our brokenness and our brightness.

First, it is totally clear to me that the heroes of the Bible had abysmal character flaws and made gross errors of judgment. From the Old Testament:

- Abraham didn't believe God's promise, took matters in his own hands, and slept with Hagar to create a son.
- Sarah laughed at God's promises.
- Moses stuttered, had a short fuse, killed a man, and questioned God's judgment in picking him.
- David killed a man and had an affair.
- Jacob was a liar and robbed his brother of his birthright.
- Jeremiah was depressed and suicidal.
- Noah got drunk.

From the New Testament:
- John was self-righteous.
- Paul spent most of his life murdering Christians.
- Peter had a bad temper and cut off someone's ear.

Nonetheless, all these people were used in amazing ways to lead a nation and change the world. And God is still using people who are broken and have failed.

Recently at church, our pastor has been going through a series called "Retrospective," exploring American culture and how public events for the last sixty years have shaped and reflected our culture. One of the media clips he used in the presentation was from Watergate. Chuck Colson was Nixon's right-hand man during the Watergate scandal and went to jail as a result. God used that experience in his life to transform the lives of thousands of people in prison over the next three decades. In Colson's own words:

> But all at once I realized that it was not my success God had used to enable me to help those in this prison, or in hundreds of others just like it. My life of success was not what made this morning so glorious—all my achievements meant nothing in God's economy. No, the real legacy of my life was my biggest failure—that I was an ex-convict. My greatest humiliation—being sent to prison—was the beginning of God's greatest use of my life; He chose the one thing in which I could not glory for His glory.

God can transform our brokenness into a reflection of His brilliance.

A while back, my daughter Tattie was reading *A Wrinkle in Time* as well as its sequel, *A Wind in the Door*. On several evenings, she asked me to read aloud to her. I was fascinated with the allegory of redemption that Madeleine L'Engle tells through her books. I was reminded of her own story of failure, which I read about in Kevin and Kay Marie Brennfleck's *Live Your Calling*. L'Engle published three books before she was thirty, then suffered a decade of failure before noting in her journal, "I'm a writer. That's who I am, even if I'm never published again." It was after this that she wrote *A Wrinkle in Time*, itself rejected thirty times before being accepted for publication and going on to win the prestigious Newbery Medal for children's literature in 1962. And here's my daughter, reading it fifty-four years later. When asked about failure, L'Engle quipped, "I've worked out a philosophy of failure which I find extraordinarily liberating. If I'm not free to fail, I'm not free to take risks, and everything in life that's worth doing involves a willingness to risk failure."

In the same way that God worked through the failures of Abraham, Moses, and Jacob to restore His nation to Himself, He worked through the failures of L'Engle and Colson to bring the message of the Gospel to children and prisoners for years to come. That should not surprise us. Romans 8:28 (NLT) clearly says: "And we know that God causes everything to work together for the good of those who love God and are called according to his purpose for them." In failure and in flaws, God works.

We should look at failure as a way of being refined, broken down, and then built back up. Failure does not define us; it's what we do with it that defines us. Sometimes we need to be cracked for the light to shine through us. I come back to this image again and again. We humans are broken vessels that try to reflect the glory of God. This idea is portrayed in 2 Corinthians 4:6–7 (NLT): "For God, who said, 'Let there be light in the darkness,' has made this light shine in our hearts so we could know the glory of God that is seen in the face of Jesus Christ. We now have this light shining in our hearts, but we ourselves are like fragile clay jars containing this great treasure."

We are called to be light as Jesus is the light. "Then spoke Jesus again to them, saying, I am the light of the world: he that follows me shall not walk in darkness, but shall have the light of life" (John 8:12, King James 2000 Bible). Through our shining, being all that we were created to be, we shed light on others: "In the same way, let your light shine before others, so that they may see your good works and give glory to your Father who is in heaven" (Matthew 5:16, ESV).

Sometimes it takes being broken for that light to shine through. This truth is not intuitive to us. We don't like to fail, and we especially do not like to fail in front of others. We often hold back. We don't freely share the talents, gifts, and skills that God has bestowed upon us through divine intervention or given us the opportunity to learn through our life experiences. We need to be transparent to be translucent. Why? So we can display God's glory. We were created to bring glory to God even in our broken state: "Bring my sons from afar and my daughters from the ends of the earth—everyone who is called by my name, whom I created for my glory, whom I formed and made" (Isaiah 43:6–7).

God is working on us. That's comforting to me. We don't have to have it all together. We don't have to get it all right. "And I am sure of this, that he who began a good work in you will bring it to completion" (Philippians 1:16, ESV). I've heard it said that failure should simply be an indication that we are under construction. Bring out the big orange cones for me! I need them. We all need them. Sometimes, we have to fail in order to truly shine.

Years ago, a friend of ours met and married a young man in our Bible study group. This gentleman was absolutely delightful and brought laughter to any room he entered. He was engaging, funny, raw, and real in his faith journey, at least what he shared with us. We adored him and we thought the two of them made a great couple. Joe and I walked them through their courtship, participated in their wedding, and cried tears of joy as they started their life together.

We then mentored this couple through the first few years of their marriage, spending countless hours together in fellowship, fun, and spiritual formation. We walked through our pregnancies together, and we were there for the birth of their first child. Just months after that child was born, however, we were devastated to learn that this gentleman was not the fabulous, faithful friend and adoring husband we thought we knew. He had been living a double life, addicted to pornography and exploits with strippers the whole time he was "building his life" with his wife. Needless to say, the marriage crumbled and he disappeared.

I was heartbroken for my friend and her infant son, whom she would be raising without his dad. In addition, I felt an incredible amount of guilt for "not seeing it." What could any of us possibly learn from this experience? I wondered, and couldn't see until recently.

Believe it or not, she turned that experience into a life's calling. At the time of her divorce, she was a high-powered international banker. It was an incredibly lucrative and glamorous job. But it was not her calling. Over the last decade, she went back to school, completed a PhD, and is now head of one of the most prestigious counseling programs in the country. Her experience has given her a perspective that she would never have known had she not gone through the pain of a broken marriage. That toxic relationship may have catalyzed her ability to bring hope and wise counsel to others. My friend is shining the light of Christ into countless marriages. God is good.

So much of my childhood was defined by hymns, songs, and choruses sung and heard in church. It's only as an adult, however, that I am truly understanding the words:

> *This little light of mine*
> *I'm gonna let it shine*
> *Hide it under a bushel—NO*
> *I'm gonna let it shine*
> *Let it shine, let it shine, let it shine!*

10

Broken

Do not be anxious about anything,
but in every situation, by prayer and petition,
with thanksgiving, present your requests to God.
And the peace of God, which passes all understanding,
will guard your heart and your mind in Christ Jesus.

Philippians 4:6

I walked into a patient's room yesterday, and I saw that the reason for the visit on the intake form simply read, "Discuss medications." I was not prepared for the conversation that ensued. I opened to door to find a petite woman I have known as a patient for years, sitting slouched in the corner of the room. Her eyes were red and puffy, and it was obvious she had been crying. She simply said, "Dr. Teague, I am in a dark place." I went on to learn that she had recently been hospitalized for four days for a suicide attempt.

She recounted the details of how her mind had been spiraling downward for several months. She started having thoughts about wanting to end the darkness and end her life. She had talked to her husband about her feelings and his response was, "Well, I don't know what to tell you." She'd scoured around the house and found a various collection of cold medicines that she'd hoped would end it all. She told me how she got as far as having the pills in her mouth and then thought about the consequences if her attempt failed. She said she did not like pain and did not want to wake up in pain. So she spit them out, called her daughter, and was taken straight to the hospital.

I was shocked. I have had the privilege to care for this patient for almost a decade. She is a banker with an excellent job. She appeared to be happily married with successful grown children. Over the years, we had treated her reflux, her insomnia, and her intermittent back pains, but I had not seen this coming. I don't think she saw the darkness approaching either. I was struck with the irony of what stopped her from killing herself: the fear of failing to do it right. She just did not want to be in pain from a failed attempt.

We talked for a while about her hospital stay. Doctors had started her on a medication in the hospital, but she said it really was not helping. In fact, she said nothing they did for her in the hospital was helpful. We worked together to find her a psychiatrist who might be a good fit for her. We talked about therapy, and a referral was made. She made a contract with me: not to act on her dark thoughts until we could work as a team to pull her out of this difficult place.

I then asked her if she was a person of faith. She said she used to be, but had not been to church in over six months. She mused that perhaps her downward spiral had something to do with that change in her habits. She had lost her connection. I reminded her that God was still there waiting for her. And God's people would welcome her back as well. I asked if I could pray for her, and her face brightened. With her hands in mine, I prayed over her the verse from Philippians that starts this chapter. We prayed for her not be anxious or depressed about anything. With prayer and petition, we presented her request for hope to God. And we asked that the peace of God that passes all understanding would guard her heart and her mind (that was in such a dark place) in Christ Jesus. We also prayed over her the promise out of Jeremiah 29:11 that says, "For I know the plans I have for you," declares the Lord, "plans to prosper you and not to harm you. Plans to give you a hope and a future." We prayed for hearty hope.

After the prayer, she looked at me with tears streaming down her face. But in her eyes, I saw hope. She thanked me and I reminded her that the promise in Jeremiah was given to the Children of Israel as they were entering the wilderness. They had forty years of wandering ahead of them. Yet that was the promise. I knew that the days ahead of her would not be easy as she sought to climb out of the pit of depression. However, I reminded her the promise stands. God has a hope and a future for her.

Her story is not unique. We are all broken, physically, emotionally, and spiritually. Most of us are trying to hold it all together, or at least look like we are holding it all together. But we are not infallible. It's amazing how open patients are to addressing spiritual things when their bodies are broken. My patient yesterday recognized that her emotional state was tied to her loss of spiritual connection. She had not only stopped going to church, she had stopped having a spiritual connection with anyone or anything.

I remember first making this connection back when I was in seminary, working at the state psychiatric hospital. It is what drew me to medicine. Profound mental and emotional illness has so many ties to the spiritual realm. I was not exaggerating when I said we had three Jesus Christs and two Virgin Marys on the same lockdown unit. When you sit with patients who are psychotic and you listen to the thoughts that are so garbled in their heads, you realize that the ability to distinguish between what is physically there and spiritually there is diminished or gone.

This spiritual brokenness has a profound impact on physical health as well. All of us, including patients, are burdened and broken. So much of physical illness is a manifestation of spiritual brokenness. And so much of our spiritual brokenness impairs our ability to physically heal. When you get past *my stomach hurts, my head hurts, I have a rash*, you often find that the real problem is something like *my sixteen-year-old has fathered a child and I have no idea how to handle it*. Sometimes, it's guilt that eats away physical health: *I had an abortion when I was seventeen and it's eating me alive. I'm forty now and a professional at the bank, but I can't let it go*. Sometimes we just cannot commit to the steps that will bring physical healing because we are stuck mentally and emotionally.

This tie of the mental, emotional, and physical is not new to medicine. There is good research that supports this codependence. There is an increased prevalence of depression in the medically ill. For example, for diseases such as heart disease, diabetes, and chronic obstructive pulmonary disease, the rates of depression range from 10–23 percent. That rate is as high as 50 percent in chronic neurological diseases such as previous stroke, Parkinson's disease or multiple sclerosis.[3] And we know that depression makes the disease process worse. There is an increase in physical complaints in diabetics, and a decrease in self-care and adherence to medical regimens.[4] Compared to a non-depressed patient, the odds are three times greater that a depressed patient would be nonadherent with medical treatment recommendations.[5] Depression even increases the number of poor choices made by diabetic patients, including increased smoking, increased body mass index, and increased Hemoglobin A1C, which is a marker of poor control.[6] Depression can also be the factor that determines life and death. Depression, for example, is associated with an increased mortality after a heart attack.[7] Our emotional health is intimately tied to our physical health.

The Scriptures are not silent on this topic. Although you won't find the word "depression" listed in the Scriptures (other than in the New Living Translation), you will find words such as downcast, sad, forlorn, afraid, troubled, discouraged, or despairing—all

3 Wayne J. Katon, "Clinical and health services relationships between major depression, depressive symptoms, and general medical illness," *Biological Psychiatry* 54, no. 3 (2003): 216-226.
4 Ludman et al., "Depression and diabetes symptom burden," *General Hospital Psychiatry* 26, no. 6 (2004): 430-436.
5 Robin DiMatteo, Heidi S. Lepper, and Thomas W. Croghan, "Depression Is a Risk Factor for Noncompliance with Medical Treatment: Meta-Analysis of the Effects of Anxiety and Depression on Patient Adherence," *Archives of Internal Medicine* 160, no. 14 (2000): 2101–07.
6 Katon et al., "Behavioral and clinical factors associated with depression among individuals with diabetes," *Diabetes Care* 27, no. 4 (2004): 914-920.
7 Nancy Frasure-Smith, François Lespérance, and Mario Talajic, "Depression Following Myocardial Infarction: Impact on 6-Month Survival," *JAMA* 270, no. 15 (1993): 1819–25.

adequately capture the definition. Repeatedly, the Scriptures point us to Him as a panacea for depression and anxiety.

So do not fear, for I am with you; do not be dismayed,
for I am your God. I will strengthen you and help you;
I will uphold my righteous right hand.

Isaiah 41:10

The Lord is close to the brokenhearted
and saves those who are crushed in spirit.

Psalm 34:18

Have I not commanded you? Be strong and courageous.
Do not be afraid; do not be discouraged,
for Lord your God will be with you wherever you go.

Joshua 1:9

And I will pray to the Father, and he shall give you another
Comforter, that he may abide with you forever.

John 14:16 (KJV)

Time after time, I have prayed that Philippians verse over my patients and pleaded for the peace of God to invade their hearts and their minds. Sometimes you know God has you exactly where he wants you when he puts patients in your path who desperately need an intervention of a higher power and a greater healer. And sometimes, God teaches you something along the way.

My journey with Otis is one of those stories.

I met Otis several years ago, when he appeared on my schedule as a new patient. I walked into the room and was immediately taken aback by the fact that he was sitting in a motorized wheelchair with two stumps for legs. Otis probably weighed 380 to 400 pounds at that point. On the ends of the stumps were bandages that looked like they had not been changed in days, if not weeks. I quickly learned that Otis had just had his second below-the-knee amputation six weeks prior. It had been done in the eastern part of the state, and he'd had no one there to care for him during his recovery. Thus, he'd "jumped" on a bus and come to Charlotte. He was staying with a distant relative and was sleeping on the floor of a stairwell on a mattress that had been dragged down the steps for him, as he could not get up the stairs.

On our first visit, my job was to clean up his wounds. The next task was to connect him with community resources and home health care to change his bandages and promote healing. As we continued to meet, I was to journey with Otis over many hills and valleys in his life. Over the next couple of years, I had lots of interactions with Otis and played many roles in his life: social worker, counselor, health coach, cheerleader, advisor, healer, friend.

Once he came into our office (after being out of care for several months due to not having any means of transportation) with severely infected stumps. As soon as he rolled off the elevator to our front office, we were called to come get him and bring him to the back as soon as possible, because his aroma was disturbing other patients. If you've ever smelled rotting flesh, you will know exactly what I'm referring to. If you haven't, imaging the most rancid scent you have ever smelled: one that brings tears to your eyes and nausea to your stomach. Multiply times ten. That's it.

My amazing staff got him back to a room and removed his prostheses. The silicone sleeves that covered his limbs and cushioned the prostheses were literally dripping with decayed material. Yet he was completely unaware of the condition of his legs. Otis is a diabetic and has a condition called neuropathy. His longstanding elevated blood sugars permanently damaged the nerves in his legs (and apparently, his olfactory nerves as well), so that he can no longer feel pain. He simply didn't realize his legs had become infected.

Otis's physical condition is akin to our spiritual condition at times. We are so accustomed to our own spiritual brokenness that we cannot even realize our needs. And we are stubborn. My grandmother used to say, "You can lead a horse to water but you can't make it drink." With a smile she'd add, "but you can feed it enough salt to make it thirsty." My job with Otis, and with all my patients, is to be the salt shaker.

I sat with Otis and explained that we had to get him to the hospital immediately. He was likely going to need surgical debridement (cleaning of the wounds) and IV antibiotics to improve his condition. He adamantly refused to go. I had used the wrong salt. After pleading with him to know the reasons why, I realized that the problem was his chair. He knew that if he was transported to the hospital via ambulance, they would not transport his motorized chair, or his prosthetic legs for that matter. This chair was his only means of transportation and there was "no way in hell" he was going to leave it! I gave him my word that we would get his chair and his legs to him at the hospital, and he agreed for us to call the ambulance. The right salt.

I kid you not when I say that my staff and I spent the next two hours trying to get his legs and his chair transported to him. I was willing to take it in my own car, but it would not fit. I called a taxi. Same problem. This chair would not fit in a regular taxi either. Finally, after a lot of begging, I convinced a social worker at the hospital to dispatch a handicap-accessible vehicle to our location. I was told, however, that they could only pull up to the curb and would not be able to come in to get the items. I work on the fifth floor of a high-rise building in the middle of downtown Charlotte, and it's not an easy option for someone to pull up to our curb! I will never forget looking out my window and seeing my registered nurse and clinical assistant driving Otis's chair and hauling those legs down to the curb! The funniest part was the trail of M&M's that fell out of the chair as they made their journey. Needless to say, Otis got his appendages, but we confiscated his M&M's.

Perhaps because of the stench or the M&M infestation, Otis needed a new chair within the next few months. Just after it was delivered, he came wheeling in to one of my exam rooms in a brand new, candy-apple-red motorized chair. He was so proud of his new ride! So proud, in fact, that he decided to do a little spin into one of my smaller exam rooms. Unfortunately, he misjudged the clearance and jammed his hand control under the countertop of my computer station. Immediately, the chair came to a screeching halt and Otis was stuck. And I do mean stuck. This was not a normal-size scooter. It was built for a person of his girth. And his girth prevented even three able-bodied caregivers from transferring him from his chair to the examination table. (Of course, on this particular day, he failed to bring in his prostheses. His new ride was so agile, he figured he did not need them. So he couldn't help us transfer, either.)

Ever tried to find a repair service for a motorized wheelchair? Me neither, until that day. Otis spent the next four hours hanging out with us in the doorway of that exam room. We bought him lunch (a healthy low-carb option, of course). We brought him magazines: every magazine in the office, to be exact. We brought him Sudoku. We played him music. And we just talked to him. Rarely in medicine do you have the opportunity to spend several hours with a patient. What a gift! Otis is amazing. Yet Otis has had his share of valleys over the years, and his physical health has trekked right along with his emotional health.

Several years ago, Otis inherited a small sum of money from a deceased relative. He promptly purchased a handicap-equipped minivan. It was, of course, candy-apple red. He brought in pictures—he was so proud! Within a few months, an estranged ex-wife appeared, and they seemed to be mending their relationship. I found myself having conversations with him around "that little blue pill" advertised on TV. Not surprisingly, Otis's health during that period was excellent. His A1C was in stellar control. He was exercising and eating well. Then, life happened. He wrecked the van, the wife left him, and he fell into a deep, dark depression. We lost him to follow-up for months on end. There were missed appointments, cancellations, and no requests for refills.

When he did reappear, his diabetes was raging out of control, which was no big surprise. His depression and despair had derailed his health. He'd just stopped caring for a while. He'd given up, become depressed. His emotional state had taken over his physical. Sound familiar? We could rewrite his insulin prescriptions, reconnect him with community resources, and renew his referral to a diabetes educator. However, what Otis really needed was divine intervention.

Prayer did more than any of the above efforts.

Even in the midst of what seem like overwhelming odds, and seasons of want and seasons of plenty, Otis showed us that you can find peace. He has no legs, no job, no home (he lives in subsidized public housing), and no family in this city. Yet over the years that I have known him, he continues to find contentment. When you ask him how he is doing, he usually smiles and says, "I am blessed." He does not worry about tomorrow. How does he do it? He gets it.

Therefore I tell you, do not worry about your life, what you will eat or drink; or about your body, what you will wear. Is not life more than food, and the body more than clothes? Look at the birds of the air; they do not sow or reap or store away in barns, and yet your heavenly Father feeds them. Are you not much more valuable than they? Can any one of you by worrying add a single hour to your life? And why do you worry about clothes? See how the flowers of the field grow. They do not labor or spin. Yet I tell you that not even Solomon in all his splendor was dressed like one of these. If that is how God clothes the grass of the field, which is here today and tomorrow is thrown into the fire, will he not much more clothe you—you of little faith? So do not worry, saying, 'What shall we eat?' or 'What shall we drink?' or 'What shall we wear?' For the pagans run after all these things, and your heavenly Father knows that you need them. But seek first his kingdom and his righteousness, and all these things will be given to you as well. Therefore do not worry about tomorrow, for tomorrow will worry about itself. Each day has enough trouble of its own.

Matthew 6:25–34

As a doctor, I can write a prescription for an antibiotic for strep throat. I can refer a patient to a surgeon for a smoldering diagnosis of gallstones. I can connect a patient with a therapist for counseling. But I cannot heal anyone. Only God brings true wholeness and healing. As the Holy Spirit leads and with the patient's permission, I routinely pray over my patients these Scriptures above and many others that I think will give spiritual healing. I can lay hands on patients and ask for God's peace. And I can pour on enough salt to make them thirsty for that healing.

11

From Mourning to Dancing

You turned my wailing into dancing; you removed
my sackcloth and clothed me with joy, that my heart may
sing your praises and not be silent. Lord my God,
I will praise you forever.

Psalm 30:11–12

So, admittedly, it had not been an easy week in the Teague
house. It started the Saturday after the holidays at the annual
cow-cutting party at my in-laws' farm. Now, before you think
really morbid thoughts about our family, let me explain.

My husband's family grows their own cattle for beef. It's not a
commercial operation; they simply keep a few cows in the family
pasture at a time. Every December or early January, they kill a few
of these cows and then gather in their own family slaughterhouse
to cut the meat. This macabre event was one of the first dates I had
with Joe more than thirty years ago—and yet somehow we kept
dating! Perhaps I come back for the social aspect of the encounter.

Every adult is expected to participate in this family-defining activity. For several years, when the boys were young, I was given a bye, as there was no one else to watch the young kids. At this point, however, the kids were old enough to roam around the farm alone, and my presence was expected and required. A few hours into the process, despite the cold temperature of the meathouse, the distinct smell of raw beef, and the messiness of the meat handling, I realized I was truly enjoying myself. Standing there hearing stories of three generations of Joe's family was utterly entertaining. They never run out of outlandish stories about growing up on the farms.

At some point two poor farming families, each with upward of ten children, lived and worked on adjacent tracts of land. Legend has it that two brothers in one family took a liking to two sisters in the other family. One sister ended up pregnant, and the presumed father disappeared. Well, that was never going to fly. An illegitimate child was not going to happen between those two farms. So a "band of brothers" took off and brought home the wayward dad. There is no proof that an actual marriage ever occurred. However, that couple was "married" over fifty years and had five children. One of those children is my father-in-law. The legacy they gave this family—one of loyalty, integrity, perseverance, justice, and laughter (lots of laughter)—is still serving them well. This family transformed an egregious error in judgment into generations of blessings. They turned mourning into dancing.

As I listened to these stories, elbow deep in cow innards, my musings on family were rudely interrupted by the sounds of wailing and pattering feet. The meathouse door flew open and there stood Tattie, bawling, hyperventilating, and babbling something along the lines of, "It's all my fault, it's all my fault . . .

I'm so sorry, Mommy, I'm so sorry, so sorry . . ." When she finally was able to catch her breath, I surmised that there had been an accident. The kids had been riding on a Gator (a six-wheeled John Deere vehicle that is a cross between a four-wheeler and a pickup truck). That fact alone was not comforting. Before she could come up with a description of "the accident," Tyre, then seven, appeared from behind her with tears streaming down his face. He opened his mouth and revealed he was missing most of his front tooth. As the story unfolded, we realized that Tattie had been driving (yeah, what's wrong with this picture so far?) and had slammed on the brakes suddenly. Tyre, riding in the bed of the Gator, had lost his balance with the sudden stop. He popped his mouth on the tailgate, and out flew his front tooth.

The next thirty minutes were a search-and-rescue mission to find the missing tooth. Two adults and five kids scrambling around knee-high grass in a pasture (with manure) trying to find one tiny, partial white tooth. Obviously, it was a hopeless and futile endeavor. We called the emergency pediatric dentist on call and he thought the tooth could wait until the next morning for repair.

Because it was the week after Christmas, I was covering other provider absences, and I had to work all day, every day that week. So Joe had the honor of taking Tyre to the dentist while I had the honor of seeing twenty-six patients, back to back. About an hour into my Monday-morning madness, I received the text photo of Tyre and his new, shiny front falsie. I hear braces don't stick to false teeth. Maybe we just saved ourselves a bill in braces for that kid, who knows? Also, I understand that false teeth don't get cavities—always looking for an upside!

As those thoughts rolled around in my head, I put down the phone on my desk and headed to the next patient room. I knew from previewing my day that this was a "heart-sink" patient (that's a nontechnical term). I have followed this patient for about eight months. The first time I met her, she was lying listless on a bed, wasted to less than ninety pounds and profoundly dehydrated. On our first encounter, I had to admit her to the hospital for severe malnutrition. Since that time, I've seen her multiple times and walked with her through numerous tests, consults and hospitalizations. I've seen her collapse on the floor in my office due to panic and an inability to manage the health issues she faces. My staff and I never know what to expect. Seeing her on my schedule gives me angst, yet hope at the same time. On many visits we have prayed together, cried together, and mourned her former self. At one point, I remember saying to her that someday we would see her dance.

I opened the door to the exam room, and there she was, waltzing around the room, literally dancing! Yes, dancing. I saw a person I did not recognize. She was smiling. Her cheeks were rosy and full. She was up to 130 pounds! Wow! The emaciated, frail shell of a woman I had met jut eight short months before was dancing in my exam room. I sat with her and wept with joy. God had turned her mourning into dancing! I walked out of that room with my heart lilting, so excited that God had worked a miracle in this woman's life. I honestly never thought she would live through that first hospitalization. There is still much illness there, and the path to wholeness is just being forged, but in her dancing, I saw hope.

My next task was to walk into my office and start wading through the messages that had accumulated from my week away. The number of messages on the screen in front of me was daunting, so I started with the ones that I thought would be easy. First, I tackled the simple refills, then I signed pending orders—making good progress. Then, I went to the lab and radiology results.

I opened the MRI result of one of my long-time patients who'd had a stable brain tumor for the last five years. The results today, however, made my heart collapse. This thirty-something-year-old mother of two boys had been diagnosed with a brain tumor in 2011. The memories of her story and her journey came flooding back to me as I read each word on the MRI report. She'd come to see me in the spring of 2011 with headaches and fatigue; she was a mother of two little ones, so fatigue and headache were no surprise! But in the midst of her work-up, she experienced a seizure, and we diagnosed her with a brain tumor.

I remember going to her head-shaving party at a salon near my house. She and her family are people of faith, and the whole process was such a blessing to me. She allowed her young boys to use the razor and shave off her hair while an army of supporting family and friends watched with tears of laughter, sorrow, and hope.

Eventually, her care had been transferred to Duke University with a team who specialized in her type of tumor. She had been on an oral chemotherapy regimen for the last two years. We ordered and followed her scans and her bloodwork here in Charlotte and then sent that information to her doctors at Duke so she didn't have to be away from her family. For years, every three months, I had the privilege of sending her a message that her labs were stable and her MRI was completely stable. That day, I did not have that privilege. Instead, I had to make a really difficult phone call informing my dear patient and friend that the once-stable, indolent tumor had exploded in the last two months.

I picked up the phone and prayed for grace and strength. The conversation, however, went nothing like I expected. She simply said, "I know." The night before, she'd had another seizure and had been seen at the emergency room. Although the MRI scan had been completed earlier in the day before the seizure, the results were still pending and she had not been informed of the results during her ER visit. She said, however, she already knew in her heart what I was going to tell her. She knew the tumor was growing again. I was expecting tears, sadness, and devastation. Instead, I heard hope and a resolve to keep fighting.

She went on to explain that she and her physicians at Duke had been talking about a new genetically targeted therapy for her type of tumor. She had not qualified for the study on this treatment, as her tumor had been quiescent. Now, she said, she might qualify for treatment, and she was thankful God had allowed this "timing" of her recurrent growth. She was sure God had a plan and purpose for this journey. Wow! That was not the response I was expecting. Our prayer together on the phone was one of hope and the desire to dance again. I hung up the phone and heard the words of Ecclesiastes 3:1: "To everything there is a season, and a time to every purpose under heaven." My patient got it.

I came home from work exhausted. I scooped up the mail in hopes of mindlessly flipping through the junk. I was entertained to see more Christmas cards trailing in. I had to chuckle; it made me feel so much better to know that I was not the only one whose Christmas cards arrived after Christmas. One card caught my attention. It was from a couple Joe and I had mentored early in their dating relationship and marriage, probably eight to ten years before.

Our church home then was a haven for millennials. Many of the individuals who attended that congregation had either never set foot in a church or had a horrible church experience at some point in their lives. We met in an old warehouse in an industrial area of Charlotte. The name of the church, Warehouse 242, reflected its mission. Acts 2:42 (NIV) describes the New Testament church: "They devoted themselves to the apostles' teaching and to fellowship, to the breaking of bread and to prayer." A warehouse is a place where something comes in, is processed, and then leaves a little different from how it arrived. The target audience for the church was people who were broken, scarred, and fragile. They needed to be processed and changed through the power of a graceful God.

This couple was no different. They had met through the church and had decided immediately to live together. Part of our counseling with them was helping them move out, live separately, and work through some issues before they did get married. Each of them had brought heavy and unwieldy baggage into the relationship. We trekked along with them during this journey of discovery of who they were and of what God's plan was for them individually and as a couple. It was a long, painful road. There were moments I thought the relationship would survive the tumult, and then there were times when I thought there was no way they would be able to work through their differences. Not long after they married, God called our family to join another church, and we left that congregation. Soon after, that couple moved away to take over the family business, and I hadn't known what had happened with them.

The postcard filled in the story. There they were, in beautiful color pictures, standing on either side of a precious red-headed little girl. The little princess was touching her mother's belly, and it was obvious that they were expecting a second. The laughter on their faces and the love in their eyes toward each other was priceless. God had redeemed them and their relationship. All I could think about was the valley they had overcome to get to that postcard.

———

At church this past week, our worship leader reminded me of the story of the blind man in John 9:1–4: "As he went along, he saw a man blind from birth. His disciples asked him, 'Rabbi, who sinned, this man or his parents, that he was born blind?' 'Neither this man nor his parents sinned,' said Jesus, 'but this happened so that the works of God might be displayed in him.'"

I thought about my husband's family. Maybe the "scandalous sin" between his grandparents happened so that God could be manifested in the legacy of his family. Maybe my patients walked through physical brokenness to experience true healing. Maybe this couple had to work through emotional baggage to experience true intimacy. I am just like the disciples following Jesus around. I immediately go to the "why" did this happen? Why does a successful professional woman "break" in her head and lose the ability to swallow? Why does a young mother get an inoperable brain cancer? Why do people hurt each other so badly in relationships? Heck, why do kids break off their front teeth? It's a question all people ask at one point or another in their lives. Why is there such suffering? Why do bad things happen to good people? Jesus's answer flips the why on its head.

Jesus says here that there is no one to blame. The *why* is not the emphasis, it's *what God can do through it*. How many of us think like that? Not me. Not naturally. Yet we need to realize that the suffering, pain, trials, and tribulations are not going to stop, at least not in this life. I roll around in the mess of people's lives all the time. At home, I answer "why" to my kids' questions over and over again: Why is that man asking for food at the stoplight? Why did those people blow up a bomb in London? Why did my guinea pig die? They are trying to make sense of their world. In the office, I weep with patients who are struggling to find answers as to why their bodies are breaking or minds are unable to process the stressors life has thrown at them. In meetings, I agonize with partners on why we cannot do the job we used to.

I am learning to stop asking why. I often reply that we are broken people and we live in a broken world. The reason for our suffering is Sin with a capital S, not the sin of a blind man. This world is groaning trying to get back to the condition that I believe it was created to be in. Through the groaning, God is trying to teach us something.

Several times in Scripture, the image of giving birth is used to illustrate the process of giving way to joy. At the end of Jesus's life, he is having a private meal with his disciples. During the course of the evening, Jesus says that he is going away for a while. Of course, they don't get it. And they immediately start asking where He is going and when He is coming back and how long they have to get along without Him. I totally get it. I would have asked the same things! We want to know how long a trial is going to last and how long we have to suffer through it. Jesus's answer ignores the matters of time and reason. His answer stresses the process and the results that follow.

> *Very truly I tell you, you will weep and mourn while the world rejoices. You will grieve, but your grief will turn to joy. A woman giving birth to a child has pain because her time has come; but when her baby is born she forgets the anguish because of her joy that a child is born into the world. So with you: Now is your time of grief, but I will see you again and you will rejoice, and no one will take away your joy. In that day you will no longer ask me anything.*
>
> John 16:20–23

Jesus makes it clear that a period of pain, sorrow, or suffering is inevitable. He does not offer to spare them from it, and the experience of pain won't feel fair. Some will be rejoicing while others are in pain.

How many times do I hear my kids exclaim in anguish, "But, Mom, that's not fair!"? (My response to which is "Give me ten push-ups or run the stairs . . . life is not fair.") Jesus does not answer the question. He says that the result is the important thing. And, oh yeah, by the way, quit asking the question! I've been through pregnancy and childbirth. I hated the whole process. But when you look at the face of your child, you forget the pain. The outcome (your child) is totally worth what it took to get there. Ironically, the exact same thing that causes the pain is the exact same thing that brings you joy!

Paul picks up this same theme in Romans. "We know that the whole creation has been groaning as in the pains of childbirth right up to the present time. Not only so, but we ourselves, who have the firstfruits of the Spirit, groan inwardly as we wait eagerly for our adoption to sonship, the redemption of our bodies" (Romans 8:22–23). Not only our physical bodies, but all of creation is groaning to get back to what we were intended to be. The process of going through the groaning can bring joy. God does not promise to replace sorrow with joy. And that's different from what we usually think. The promise of Jesus and of the Scriptures is that God can take the very thing that causes the pain and sorrow and bring joy. I see this in my own children. I see this in the lives of my patients. I have seen this in the aftermath of the devastation of the earthquake in Haiti in 2010. This is a revelation of one of the great principles that marks authentic faith, one of the ways God works in our lives. He takes the things that break our bodies, minds, and spirits, and turns them into a cause of joy.

James 1:2–4 (MSG) says, "Consider it a sheer gift, friends, when tests and challenges come at you from all sides. You know that under pressure, your faith-life is forced into the open and shows its true colors. So don't try to get out of anything prematurely. Let it do its work so you become mature and well-developed, not deficient in any way." Wow. That's a hard truth to swallow. But I get it, even if I don't fully understand it. I hear it when I call to tell a young mother her brain tumor is raging out of control and find that she is at peace with that knowledge. I see it when a patient I thought would die is dancing across a room. And I feel it when my kid crawls on my lap to tell me she loves me after I've had to discipline her for wrecking a Gator and breaking a tooth.

I'm trying to be God's instrument of healing and hope. Isaiah, in chapter 61:1–3, describes Jesus's role in the world. I want to be Jesus to my family, my patients, and my partners. This is my paraphrased prayer:

> *Dear Lord, please place your Spirit upon me to bring good news to the sick and afflicted, to bind up the brokenhearted, to show freedom to those whose spirits are bound, to comfort those who mourn, to give a garland of gladness to those who carry a burden of pain, and to exchange a cloak of oppression for a mantle of praise. Help me point others to the one who can turn their mourning to dancing.*

12

Reset and Recharge

*The King will reply, "Truly I tell you, whatever you did for one of
the least of these brothers and sisters of mine, you did for me."*

Matthew 25:40

Friday was one of those days in the office when I knew another
set of feet had carried me through the day. I don't know how I
would have gotten through it otherwise.

My first patient was in for a simple six-month checkup. But
when my nurse came out and said, "Something's wrong with
his heart rate," I realized there would be nothing "simple" about
the visit. I walked in to find a generally well sixty-five-year-old
gentleman in a crazy cardiac arrhythmia. He had enough cardiac
risk factors, including hypercholesterolemia and hypertension,
to let me know that I should not ignore this finding. An EKG
confirmed the abnormality, and he was quickly scheduled to go in
for a stress test.

Needless to say, that fifteen-minute visit warped into forty-five minutes, and I was behind for the rest of the day. I pride myself on staying on time, but after that I walked into every room apologizing for being a few minutes late. At one point, I exited an exam room to see another patient standing half-clad in a gown at the doorway of his room, looking up and down the hall, eagerly awaiting my arrival to his room. By that point, I had made up a lot of time and was only fourteen minutes off schedule. Still, I was embarrassed and frustrated to be so late.

I had no time for a lunch break, so I scarfed down a few bites of what I'd packed from home in between seeing patients. By three thirty, I was completely spent. But when I walked in to see my second-to-last patient of the day, I was blown away.

Ruth is a middle-aged woman I have followed for over ten years. She is one of my favorites. I suppose as a doctor you're not supposed to have favorites, but she always makes me smile and reminds me of why I do what I do.

It would be an understatement to say Ruth has had a difficult life. To my knowledge, she never finished high school. Her literacy level is low and her health literacy even lower. She has been morbidly obese for most of her life. She's had little medical care, other than for the birth of her children, before she started seeing me. She's worked in minimum-wage jobs most of her life. Her diet reflected the choices made by those who have limited resources— fast foods and cheap carbs. A commenter on the Freakonomics blog called the McDonald's McDouble "the cheapest, most nutritious and bountiful food that has ever existed in human history." Sadly, the commenter is right; such foods are a quick and easy choice for patients like Ruth.

All those circumstances culminated in Ruth being obese

and having poorly controlled diabetes. By the time she became my patient, she was struggling with damage to her eyes. She was deemed legally blind early in our relationship. Thus, she lost her ability to drive and her assembly line job. Nevertheless, she did not give up her desire to work, and found a job in food services in our public school system. She truly loved the kids, but she'd tell me stories of how they made fun of her for being fat and ugly. She is neither, on the outside or the inside. She is one of the most beautiful people I have ever met.

Each time she comes to my office, she greets me with a smile and a hug and tells me how thankful she is for all that I have done for her. She always asks about my children and what is happening in my life. She remembers to ask about my vacations. She remembered to ask about the recent construction project we had at our house. She even remembers my birthday.

On Friday, she greeted me with more than her precious smile.

I walked into the room, and after her sweet greetings, she insisted that I sit down. She wanted to give me something. On top of my computer sat a very large gift bag with brightly colored tissue paper peeking out of the top. She insisted that I open the bag before we got down to her exam. At the top of the bag was a tray of neatly wrapped homemade cookies. She wanted me to share them with the whole office and thank them for everything they have done for her over the years. She was very proud to let me know the cookies had been made with Splenda, not sugar. She wanted me to know she was making much better choices and taking better care of herself.

Under the cookies was a small burlap bag filled with sweet-smelling toiletries and bath salts. She said she knew that I always seemed to be working too hard and I needed to do something for myself. She wanted me to go home, pour a nice bath, and relax for a few minutes. I chuckled; she had me nailed, because I don't take time for myself. I couldn't remember the last time I'd sat in a tub to relax!

After another layer of tissue paper, there was yet another surprise in the bag. I reached in and pulled out an absolutely gorgeous handmade afghan, perfectly matching the colors of the bedroom we had just added to our home. With tears streaming down my face, I looked at her in disbelief. She smiled and reminded me that she'd asked about my new addition and the colors I had chosen in my bedroom at our last visit. She had then crocheted an afghan for my new room. She wanted me to curl up under it with my husband and be reminded of how much I was loved by her and my patients.

I sat there in the room and just wept. I didn't know what to say. This legally blind woman had spent her own money to make gifts so heartfelt and kind. She then prayed with me. She asked God to give me grace and wisdom as I sought to do his work as an instrument in healing.

When we finally got around to addressing her needs and the reason for her visit, she recounted how she had called ten or twelve dental facilities in the area and was unable to find a place to have several of her front teeth extracted. Years of poor dental care were taking their toll, and she had multiple teeth that needed to go. She had been given three or four rounds of antibiotics to try to keep the pain at bay until she could get these teeth extracted. Even if she went to one of the cash-only clinics, she was unable to muster $175 for the extraction. I looked at the bag of goodies she'd brought to me and was overwhelmed. She'd spent her own money for the groceries to make the cookies, the toiletries to give me a break, and the yarn to create this afghan, and yet here she needed the money for her painful teeth.

I spent the next four days trying to get her the dental care that she needed. Dental care for indigent patients in our city is abysmal! But thanks to the perseverance of my staff, she will eventually get her extractions.

When I finally got home that evening, I sat and thought about the events of the day. Despite the rocky start, the unexpected cardiac emergency, the irritation of my tardiness to see twenty-plus patients, and utter mental exhaustion, God showed up in Ruth's presence that day. And He smacked me across the face with His goodness. I heard him echo again to me, "What you have done for the least of these, you've done for me." He blesses.

You would think that I could remember that. But I forget. A lot. The stresses of being a doctor in the world of heath-care reform make it really hard to remember.

———

Did you know that your doctor now gets a report card? It's true. I just got off the phone from an hour-long conference call reviewing the "quality metric data" for every internal medicine provider over whom I have responsibility. Who gives the report cards? The government. The insurance companies. The outside purveyors of health-care quality. Everyone who has anything to do with health care. What are we graded on? How about readmission rates, or the percentage of our patients who are readmitted within thirty days of an illness? How about prevention metrics, including the percentage of our patients who get appropriate preventive screenings, based on age and gender, such as pap smears, colonoscopies, and mammograms? How about chronic disease management, such as the control metrics for disease like diabetes or congestive heart failure? Yep, they are all included in the report cards. Once a patient establishes care with me, after just one visit, I am held responsible for meeting a veritable plethora of quality metrics for that patient, as well as all others for whom I am listed as the primary care physician, for the next eighteen months. Reimbursement from third-party payers (such as the government and insurance companies) is tied to these metrics. Thus, my paycheck is tied to those grades as well. I am paying attention.

Since 2010, the Affordable Care Act has provided the opportunity for over 20 million Americans to enroll in a type of health insurance (including Medicaid, the ACA Marketplace, and children staying on their parents' plans).[8] Many of these individuals have not had any interaction with a doctor in years. Their health literacy is very low. They have had no preventive screenings, and they have diseases that are raging out of control due to lack of health care. Providing care to these folks can be demoralizing, overwhelming, and humbling, as many don't understand that getting appropriate screenings or following a doctor's advice is important. Or else it's difficult for them to make health care a priority in between balancing jobs, childcare, and paying the bills. Often, they are choosing between food and health care. Yet we, as providers, are held responsible for their care. We are graded on doing the right

---

8 Obamacarefacts.com, July 27, 2016.

thing for these and all of our patients. *We* are held responsible for the individual choices the *patients* are making. Sadly, "bad grades" given to providers can be dis-incentivizing to offer care to those who need it most.

I met Sarah a few months ago. The chief reason for her visit: "medication refills." That complaint could not have been more inaccurate, and I was not prepared for the first few minutes I spent in her exam room. My nurse had stepped into another room before I entered Sarah's room, so I was not given a heads-up about what to expect. As I peeked in the door, I was greeted by a fifty-eight-year-old, morbidly obese African American patient, sitting on the table. At 450 pounds and five foot two, she was about three times her ideal body weight. She was crying. The next few minutes involved her spilling her story of being depressed and alone. She explained that she was not married and had estranged children. She was not involved in any community activities and worked in a low-paying hourly wage job. She felt she had no friends and no one to talk to when she came home from work. She denied wanting to harm herself or anyone else, but she said she just had no hope. I offered a prayer and encouraged her to seek a faith community, even if she had never found one before.

Once we got past the tears, I asked about her physical health. She took no medication, as she had not seen a physician in fifteen or twenty years—probably since the birth of her children. At some point, she had been told she had high blood pressure and had been given medication for that. But that prescription had long since expired, and she had no idea if the problem still existed. She just knew that she did not feel well and decided that since she now had insurance (thanks to the Affordable Care Act, aka Obamacare), she needed to come to a doctor.

I glanced at her vital signs; her blood pressure was 180/120, almost into stroke range. She was completely asymptomatic, though, and I surmised that her blood pressure had likely been that high for a really long time. I asked if she had tried any lifestyle modifications for managing her blood pressure in the past, such as decreasing her sodium intake, or exercising for health. She said she had no time for exercise because she works twelve-hour shifts. When I asked her if she had any physical symptoms, she said she was thirsty all the time, tired, and her feet were numb and painful at the same time: a sure sign of diabetes. When I asked what she was drinking, she stated she drank about two gallons of sweet tea a day! That's more than enough sugar to kill anyone. Her job was in food services at a local nursing home, and sweet tea was available to her all day, every day.

I asked my nurse to step in and do a quick screen for diabetes. That test, known as a glycosylated hemoglobin A1C, came back at 14.6 percent. This indicated that her blood sugar had been around 400 for at least three months. (Just for the record, the normal blood-sugar range is 70–120 with an A1C of less than 5.6 percent.) Translation: This patient had long-standing, poorly controlled diabetes. That certainly would explain increased thirst and exhaustion. And the constant onslaught of sweet tea would explain the worsening symptoms, as the nerve endings in her feet and elsewhere were being damaged from the high sugar in her blood.

I introduced the idea of trying some lifestyle modifications (cutting out the sweet tea and drinking water instead, aiming for a healthier diet, and walking more) as well as two very inexpensive medications (easily attainable on the $4 list at Walmart), one for the diabetes and one for the elevated blood pressure. She replied that I was welcome to write my prescriptions, but she would not get paid for another two weeks, and there was no way she could purchase any medications until then. I so wanted her to start on those medications straightaway!

At that point she looked at me and, with tears in her eyes, pleaded, "Now that I know all these things are wrong with me, there is no way I can work. Can you just write me a note to be permanently disabled?"

I felt so frustrated and defeated that I didn't know what to do. It's like being sucker punched in the gut. The determination of disability is a complicated process through the Department of Social Security and your insurance carrier. That process starts, however, with a physician's determination that a patient is unable to work or hold a permanent job due to his or her health status. I was meeting this patient for the first time. There was no way I could make that determination on one visit or one thirty-minute assessment.

This frustration is what my colleagues in medicine are feeling all the time. My patient, like so many others, desperately needed health care. And I desperately wanted to help her feel better and be healthier. But her agenda was going on permanent disability. Sadly, this patient never returned to my clinic. She missed her follow-up appointments. We called. We sent letters. And we got no response. She is, however, still my responsibility. I will be graded on my performance of her health for the next eighteen months. My paycheck is tied to that grade as well. She is due for multiple health maintenance screenings (mammogram, pap smear, colonoscopy), so based on Sarah's current statistics, I am flunking. I get labeled a bad doctor. Do you remember my grandmother's wisdom about leading a horse to water and feeding him enough salt to make him thirsty? Well, I have not had the chance to pour enough salt on this patient to make her thirsty. I needed more time, and now I'm afraid she'll never come back and will get more and more sick.

That day I met Sarah, I left work completely forlorn and upset. I have learned, however, that when my spirit is weary and I'm questioning why I do what I do, God shows up and hits the reset button.

The same is true for technology. I jokingly say that I don't know where I'm going unless I check my external brain, i.e., my Outlook calendar on my iPhone. We had a time change recently, and something horrific happened to my calendar. All my recurrent standing meetings got shifted by an hour. I started getting all these messages about appointments that were in conflict with other appointments on my calendar. I called Information Services for help. No one could seem to understand what had happened. I tried the reset button and that did not work. Eventually, I decided to plug the phone into the desktop, wipe all the programs clean, and reload them all. Guess what? It worked!

Sometimes, I think God has to do that for me and for the practice of medicine. Sometimes God sends patients like Ruth to reset my soul. Sometimes He needs to pull me out of my comfort zone to get my attention. I have to be wiped clean, plugged into the Source, and reset.

———

I mentioned before that I feel like my mission field is a ten-by-ten examination room. I would be lying, however, if I did not admit that for years my heart longed to go outside this country and be on the real mission field I'd read about when I was a kid growing up in that Southern Baptist Church. I had spent a few months in Kenya at the end of medical school before starting residency, and since then, I'd been itching to go back. But when you have four children under the age of ten, it's hard to go to the mission field. I started praying about heading back to the field, and, as usually happens, God showed up through a series of coincidences.

I went to a business meeting with my boss to try to learn how to recruit physicians for a local mission opportunity. Instead of recruiting some of my colleagues, they recruited me! I found myself committing to go to Haiti with an organization called Bless Back Worldwide. BBW was founded in 2010, right after the devastating earthquake in Haiti. A group of local providers from Charlotte went to Haiti to provide aid within a few weeks of the natural disaster. They quickly realized, however, that the people of Haiti needed more than relief. They need development. Thus, BBW was born as an organization that goes in and supports local organizations striving to better the lives of the people in their communities.

When I committed to the trip, I tried to educate myself on the local history and politics of Haiti. Since the earthquake in 2010, billions of dollars have been poured into that country. When I arrived in 2015, I expected to see the early fruits of regeneration, regrowth, and rebirth. I was not prepared for what hit me at the airport. I was face-to-face with deprivation and abject poverty in a way that I had never been. Working with the Maasai people of Kenya, who chose tribal living over the advances of modern living, was one thing. Working with people whose lives had been devastated by a natural disaster not of their own choosing was another. We drove through open sewers where the stench of human excrement and rotting trash was stifling. We saw rows and rows of tent dwellings (four posts, a tin roof, wrapped in Samaritan's Purse blue tarps, that had been built through aid projects in 2010 and never replaced with sturdier dwellings). We visited villages where half-naked children eagerly scarfed down our deworming treatments just to get the granola bar that chased it down. All of it was shocking.

I volunteered in a clinic where I saw patient after patient whose lives had been adversely affected by the earthquake and tsunami five years before. One of the physician's assistants traveling with us came over to my bay and asked me to come see an infant with her. Mind you, I am NOT a pediatrician, and part of the challenge for me on this trip was seeing kids suffering so terribly. I was way out of my comfort zone. I walked over to see a morbidly obese baby who was probably eight to ten months old. The young mother had never sought medical attention for her child, who had been born at home. Over the course of the next five minutes, we realized that child was blind and deaf. This new mother had absolutely no idea that anything was wrong with the child. Through the translator, she admitted that he was often fussy so she fed him continuously to soothe him. That explained his large girth. I picked up this baby, held him close to my heart, and just wept.

I had to tell this young mother, with the help of the Creole translator, that her child could not see nor hear, and likely never would. Perhaps my heart was raw to this child because I had just walked with my first nanny through the birth of her child, who was born with significant disabilities. In the States that child was immediately identified as needing help and surrounded by an army of speech therapists, physical therapists, and medical professionals who could help my nanny get her child the services needed. This Haitian mother had but a few family members to help. There was a physical therapist coming on the next team of volunteers, and I was able to connect her with the mom. She could help her with some simple exercises to increase sensory stimuli for this baby. My services to her, however, were woefully inadequate. Perspective is everything.

I wiped my tears and walked back to my cubicle to see my next patient. The elderly Haitian woman appeared to be thin and frail, but her age was difficult to guess. Most of these folks did not know their birthdays, as age to them was not important. She was brought in by a distant relative who indicated the woman had been widowed. Through the Creole translator, the woman described the sensation of "fire in her belly" and "a knife" in her upper abdomen. I was thinking she might have reflux, but I wanted to clarify the diagnosis with questions. I asked, "Is the pain worse when you eat?" There was a long silence and the lady looked at the ceiling and around the room.

Finally, she looked at the translator and answered, "I don't know because I don't eat very often."

I found myself choking back tears once again. Somehow, I did not think my prescription for an acid suppressant would help this woman. First, I prayed with her, and then I was able to connect her with a food service sponsored by the World Health Organization, where she could come in once a month and get a package of food. The program was intended for children, but I didn't think the WHO would mind if one starving, elderly lady took a package home too.

I practice medicine in the most technologically advanced medical system in the world. Yet only a three-hour plane ride away, widows are starving, families are homeless, and children are born without their basic needs for food, shelter, and clothing met. While many in our inner city of Charlotte have the same needs, in the midst of these needs, whether in Haiti or right here at home, I see God at work. I understand what Isaiah was trying to say:

Then said I, Woe is me! I am undone;
because I am a man of unclean lips, and I dwell
in the midst of a people of unclean lips:
for mine eyes have seen the King, the Lord of hosts.

Isaiah 6:5 (KJV)

I get the amazing opportunity to see God show up in the midst of great pain, suffering, and need. It is amazing how open we are to address spiritual things when our bodies and minds are broken. I was unplugged and reset in Haiti. I am going back again in just a few months. I need to be reminded, over and over again, what it means to care for the least of these. I want to be faithful to care for God's children, Ruth and Sarah, the Haitian widow and the infant. I want to hear the King reply to me, "What you did for the least of these, you did for me."

13

Just Because We Can
Doesn't Mean We Should

The Lord brings death and makes alive;
he brings down to the grave and raises up.

1 Samuel 2:6

We have our priorities all screwed up when it comes to medicine in the United States. We confuse quantity with quality, and we have no idea how to die with dignity. Before you judge me for being completely morbid, hear me out.

I was first convinced about this issue in medical school. I was blessed to train at a huge teaching hospital, UNC Hospitals. As a teaching institution, we were the referral center for the region. As with any teaching institution that leverages the "free labor" of medical students and residents, we cared for all God's children: the poor, the undocumented immigrants, the illiterate. I realized that often we performed procedures and initiated treatments not because it was the right thing for the patients, but because we operated on the premise of prolonging life, no matter what the cost financially, emotionally, or physically to the patient. As a medical student, I was not in a position to make a lot of decisions. I just watched. And I questioned (to myself) what we were doing. Why did we perform seemingly futile surgeries on ninety-year-old patients? Why did we continue chemotherapy when it clearly was not working? Why did we pursue a full code and initiate all forms of life support on patients whose illness had already stripped them of life?

I was so burdened by this topic that I wanted to learn more. The question inspired my medical school honors thesis on end-of-life issues. I had the opportunity to study the medical literature filtered through my study of the Scriptures. And this exploration was sifted through my belief in the sanctify of life as a gift from God. The research clearly showed that providing "nutrition" through tube feedings and fluids through IVs prolonged life. However, the consequences were often devastating for the patient. Death was delayed, but "life" was not pleasant. Patients often suffered aspiration pneumonias and died from "drowning" as their lungs filled with fluid. We created the suffering of aspiration with the feeding tubes. Yet we still did it!

I realized that our medical ability to "do something" far outstripped our medical ethics to know how and when to use medical interventions. Just because we can does not mean that we should.

The consequences of this ethical dilemma are devastating. Countless statistics show that we spend more and more money, resources, and time trying to gain quantity than we do to ensure quality. From 2002 to 2010, the per capita health-care spending for those between ages 65 and 84 grew 36 percent, and for those older than 85, spending grew 38 percent.[9] Of the 6 percent of Medicare patients who die each year, 27–30 percent of Medicare costs are attributed to them. Does this make sense? I would argue that it does not. And it's not about the money. It's about the prolonged suffering that we create. Ian Morrison, an internationally known author, consultant, and speaker specializing in long-term forecasting with an emphasis on health care, stated the problem well: "Patients, families, and providers are ill-equipped to have the candid, open dialogue about preferences, probabilities, and planning for the end. Instead, all too often, physicians 'do their best' or 'do everything they can' but still come up short of preventing mortality, while in many cases aggravating morbidity and eroding the quality of life remaining."

In residency, you have more time to spend with patients than the attending physicians do (because you're pretty much living at the hospital for about three years)! I decided to take that time to truly get to know my patients and their families. When you do that, you can have real and meaningful conversations. One conversation has stayed with me for years.

I was the Internal Medicine resident on call for the Medical ICU, and I was called to the Emergency Department (ED) to admit a patient who was very unstable. I remember running to the ED and trying to quickly assess the situation. The twenty-something-year-old woman had a fever, was tachycardic (rapid heart rate), and her blood pressure was requiring IV medication to keep her alive. It was clear she was septic, meaning she had a diffuse infection in

9 Ian Morrison, PhD, "Health Care Costs and Choices in the Last Years of Life," *Hospitals & Health Networks*, March 3, 2015.

her blood. We just did not know at the time what was causing it. When I walked into the room, she was still awake and crying from fear. There was a bustle of activity around her, nurses drawing blood, others placing IVs in her arms, radiology technicians taking x-rays of her chest. Her mother and father were at her bedside, equally distraught, not knowing what to say or what to ask.

Over the next few minutes, it became apparent to us that this young woman needed to be placed on a ventilator, because her lungs were filling with fluid and she was not breathing well. I leaned in close to her face and told her what was about to happen. I promised her that I would be there when she awakened. Then I prayed with her and her family. I prayed that when she awakened, it would be in this world and not the next one.

The next several weeks were touch-and-go. The infection, which ended up being from a rare bacteria, ravaged her body. Her kidneys failed, and she was placed on dialysis. She lost the ability to regulate intravascular fluids and her body swelled to twice its normal weight. Her circulation failed, and several toes and part of a foot had to be amputated as the infection raged. Every day, I was at her bedside with her family. We cried together, we hoped together, we prayed together. Together, we struggled and talked through many decisions on what treatment to pursue next, on what treatments to avoid, and on what this young woman would have wanted, as she could not speak for herself. On more than one occasion, I had to tell this family that we had nothing more to offer medically. The Giver and Taker of life was in charge. We walked through the Valley of the Shadow of Death together.

It was not her time to go. I was there the day we awakened her and pulled the ventilator tube from her lungs. And she smiled at me. She thanked me for being there, just like I said I would be.

She lived and is now thriving as a wife, a mother of two, and an agent of positive change as a medical social worker. Her picture still sits in my office. I have the honor to now care for her family. Because I dared to have those hard conversations with her family, because I listened, because I sought to understand what was important to them, they have chosen to follow me into practice. What an amazing blessing!

I had thought that all physicians had these same conversations with their patients, but I was wrong. I watched my own colleagues in residency struggle to talk about life and death with their patients. By the end of residency, I was known by my classmates as "the grim reaper." Why? Because death did not scare me, and I was willing to walk through that valley with patients. On many occasions, I was paged by one of my classmates asking me to come "have the talk" with a family when they could not do it themselves. "The talk" is the difficult conversation you must have with a family when your medical tools may prolong life, but they will not restore the person back to the mother, father, child, or spouse that they once were.

According to a RAND study, one in ten patients receive ICU care that is considered futile by their treating physician, and more than two-thirds of them die during their hospitalizations.[10]

One eighty-two-year-old matriarch was "found down" in her home by one of her eight children. By the time she arrived at the hospital, her brain images revealed that she'd had a massive

10 Catherine Winters, "Critical Care May Not Always Be the Right Choice," LiveScience, September 9, 2013.

hemorrhagic stroke. One half of her brain was compromised by the bleed. En route to the hospital, she had been intubated and resuscitated, a default treatment by emergency medical services. She was placed in the neurosurgery ICU, and a drain had been placed in her skull to relieve the pressure on her brain. Weeks passed. Her brain stem was still functioning, allowing her heart to beat, but her cognitive abilities were gone.

This woman was not ever going to recover. Yet she was kept alive, at the cost of about $11,000 per day.[11] Six of the eight children were ready to say good-bye, and then an estranged daughter arrived. She adamantly refused to turn off life support for her mother. I was paged to help the family.

I learned that this daughter and the mother had had a falling out years before. The daughter was not ready to let go, as she had never reconciled their differences. The siblings had shunned this daughter due to her life choices and the dispute she'd with their mother. The conversation was painful. There were expletives. There was slander. There were colorful names attributed to one another. And there were tears. Lots of tears.

Hours later, there was healing, restoration, and hope. Not only was there an agreement to let their mother go, but there was also a commitment to rebuild and restore relationships. Why? Because we were willing to talk about life, death, pain, suffering, and priorities. I felt like I was in seminary all over again as we explored the age-old questions of faith, such as why a good God would allow bad things to happen, in the midst of experiencing profound loss

11 Joseph F. Dasta, Trent P. McLaughlin, and Samir H. Moody, "Daily cost of an intensive care unit day: The contribution of mechanical ventilation," *Critical Care Medicine* 33, no. 6 (2005): 1266-71.

and grief. Amazing how things come full circle.

We are blessed in the US to have a phenomenal National Hospice and Palliative Care Organization that coordinates thousands of local groups facilitating compassionate care for people facing life-limiting illnesses. They focus on caring, not curing. The first Hospice program opened in 1974. Currently, there are 6,100 programs in fifty states, the District of Columbia, Puerto Rico, Guam, and the US Virgin Islands. According to their statistics from 2014, 35.5 percent of patients pass away within seven days and 50.3 percent within fourteen days of admission to Hospice.[12] I would argue that more of our health care should focus on caring and not curing, and we should be lengthening the time between Hospice enrollment and death so that we focus on compassionate care for longer than just the last few weeks of life.

I have tried to carry this passion for honoring life into my practice as an internist for the last fifteen years. If you come to see me, I'll ask you if you have a living will or health-care power of attorney. If you don't, I'll encourage you to get one. I will encourage you to ponder death while you are full of life. Death is a natural part of life. If you face the reality that your body, at some point, will not function the way it does now, you can make choices about how you may want to spend your last days. Facing the fear of death gives you a sense of control. None of us know from what cause or when we will die, but we may be able to affect how we leave this world. I think my patients appreciate my willingness to face that reality with them.

12 *NHPCO's Facts and Figures: Hospice Care in America*, 2015 edition, National Hospice and Palliative Care Organization.

About eight years ago, just a few years after I started practice, I was covering clinic for one of our senior physicians away on sabbatical. That day, I met a chipper elderly man who came in complaining of bright red blood with a recent bowel movement. In taking the history, I learned he'd had also had some weight loss, some fatigue, and a general lack of "spunk" over the last few months. Red flags went up for me; I was concerned he could have cancer. I am really not sure exactly what I said to the patient and his wife that day, but I know I was honest. I told them that I was concerned about finding cancer and how we needed to proceed with testing to confirm or rule out this diagnosis. They acknowledged that they understood the plan and thanked me for my candor. We prayed. I challenged them to set priorities and be prepared for whatever path lay ahead.

This sweet gentleman was diagnosed with gastrointestinal cancer and passed away within three months of his visit. I kept up with them through that time, but I was not the primary care physician for the patient.

Several years later, I walked in to an exam room with a chart that just read "new patient, establish care." I entered the room and was greeted with a hug. The sweet lady asked if I remembered her. I knew the face but not the name. She recounted how I had been the doctor who told her husband that he had cancer. She explained how my compassion and candor with them that day had made an indelible impression. She told me that she and her husband had a beautiful three months together after that day of diagnosis, because we had been willing to talk about death. When her primary care physician retired (she had seen the same physician as her husband), she told him there was only one other doctor she would see. She had driven thirty miles to see me. That was five years ago, and she is still my patient. She spends half the year on Cape Cod and half the year in North Carolina. Yet she "commutes" to see me. Why? Because I was willing to engage her and her beloved husband in a conversation about how they wanted to spend the rest of their life together. Wow! What a blessing.

Atul Gawande's book *Being Mortal* documents the dilemma of addressing mortality with patients. In his words: "We've been wrong about what our job is in medicine. We think our job is to ensure health and survival. But really it is larger than that. It is to enable well-being. And well-being is about the reasons one wishes to be alive. Those reasons matter not just at the end of life, or when debility comes, but all along the way."

I have been saying this for years, and I am still saying it and trying to live this out with my patients. I don't know how Dr. Gawande derives his peace with discussing the end of life with his patients. He is a surgeon. For surgeons, "to cut is to cure." I am an internist. We know that we do not often cure anything. Internists are known as "fleas," which are the last things to leave a dying organism. I am not sure this was ever intended as a compliment, but I have chosen to take it as one in my career. Last I checked, we all have a 100 percent chance of dying.

The Scriptures are pretty clear on our source of life and our mortality. "And the Lord God formed man of the dust of the ground, and breathed into his nostrils the breath of life; and man became a living soul." (Genesis 2:7 (KJV)). Ecclesiastes 12:7 says, "So, our bodies return to the earth, and the life-giving breath returns to God." We don't live forever. In fact, Satan's first lie in the Bible occurs in Genesis 3:4, when the serpent says to the woman, "You will not surely die." But of course that's wrong: we all do. And the Bible even clearly delineates our anticipated age. "Our days may come to seventy years, or eighty, if our strength endures; yet the best of them are but trouble and sorrow, for they quickly pass, and we fly away." (Psalm 90:10). I find this amazingly prescient. Since the time of David, our mortality has been pretty much set. Given all our scientific knowledge, understanding of disease processes, and clinical acumen of diagnosis and treatment of common illnesses, we still have not been able to extend life. Current 2015 life expectancy statistics suggest men in the US live about seventy-seven years, women about eighty-two.[13]

In cellular biology class, I studied the concept of the Hayflick limit. In the early 1960s, Hayflick and Moorhead showed that human cells do not divide indefinitely, but reach a limit of replication and stop all further division. This is known as the Hayflick limit. This limitation of division is genetically programmed into cells by specific genes. The language of life, DNA, choreographs cell aging. When cells are damaged, these same genes should lead to cell suicide, known as apoptosis, or dormancy. If that process does not work, damaged cells replicate uncontrollably. This immortal cellular state is known as cancer! Aging mammalian cells are programmed to stop dividing and enter dormancy, or undergo apoptosis, if they are damaged by environmental insults. This process protects us from tumor formation, or cancer. This same DNA language also limits our cellular lifespan.[14] Again, I am

13 *World Population Prospects: Key findings and advance tables*, 2015 Revision, United Nations Department of Economic and Social Affairs Population Division, New York: United Nations, 2015.
14 L. L. May Hoopes, "Aging and Cell Division," *Nature Education* 3, no. 9

blown away by this intelligent design. But I am also reassured that death of our cells (and us) is a beautifully choreographed part of a divine plan.

We should face aging and mortality with grace. We need to honor the aging process, not necessarily try to stop it. Although I admittedly color those gray roots now and again, I want to embrace the wisdom of Proverbs 16:31: "Gray hair is a crown of splendor; it is attained by a righteous life." We have to learn to let go and face the reality that our bodies are not designed to live forever.

Just this week, I had an office visit with a woman in her late forties, whom I've been seeing for years. The reason for this visit was a follow-up on recent labs and her complaint of "not feeling well." Every lab was normal. Yet she was convinced something was wrong with her. Ultimately the conversation came back to the reality of just being a forty-eight-year-old. She asked for a referral to a plastic surgeon for a tummy tuck, a referral to a dermatologist for Botox, and a referral to a naturopathic provider to try those "bioidentical hormones." I explained that the only success of these referrals would be weight loss to her wallet! But she was willing to pay for it all in an effort to stay young. The global anti-aging market is poised to grow 7.8 percent between 2013 and 2019. It is estimated that baby boomers will spend $191.6 billion to ward off aging by 2019.[15] Nope, many of us are not going gently into that good night, and are willing to lay down money to ward off the

---

(2010): 55.

15 "Anti-aging Market (Anti-wrinkle products, Hair Color, Hair restoration treatment, Breast augmentation and Radio frequency devices)—Global Industry Analysis, Size, Share, Growth, Trends and Forecast, 2013–2019," January 14, 2014, http://www.transparencymarketresearch.com/anti-aging-market.html.

inevitable!

I think my job as a physician is to illuminate the process of aging and the inevitability of death with humility, honesty, and hope. I want to have candid conversations with patients about death while we are full of life. I cannot give life. I cannot take it, either. Only God can do that. But I do know the Giver and the Taker of life. And I know from where my peace with passing comes: "Yea, though I walk through the valley of the shadow of death, I will fear no evil: for thou art with me; thy rod and thy staff they comfort me." (Psalm 23:4, KJV)

May I always walk this path with grace.

14

The Importance of Speaking Life

*Let no unwholesome word proceed from your mouth, but only
such a word as is good for edification according to the need of the
moment, so that it will give grace to those who hear.*

Ephesians 4:29 (New American Standard Version)

*The tongue has the power of life and death,
and those who love it will eat its fruit.*

Proverbs 18:21

*Those who guard their mouths and their
tongues keep themselves from calamity.*

Proverbs 21:23

What we say has such a powerful influence on everyone in
our realm. God referred to Himself as the Word in John

1:1. This has profound implications for us and how we use our own words. Spoken language has weighty connotations for understanding the DNA language of life. Words are powerful: they can build up or tear down. In all my roles, I know that how I speak has the most profound influence on all that I do. Sometimes I get it right. Sometimes I fail miserably.

I distinctly remember the first words spoken to me that opened my eyes to this concept.

One hot summer Sunday night when I was six, I listened to a pastor talking about Jesus standing at the door of my heart and knocking. Those words painted a picture in my head of something I had never grasped before. I stopped eating the crackers from the grandmothers who flanked me on that church pew that night, and sat perfectly still. It suddenly hit me that Jesus was talking to me. I could feel Him. Through those words, I could see him knocking at the door of my heart. I sensed Him saying that he wanted to be a part of my life.

Even at six, I understood. I'd heard all those Bible stories. I knew what it meant to realize I was messed up inside. But I had no idea what to do. I'm sure there were twelve stanzas of "Just As I Am" as I stood there fidgeting the whole time, so wanting to move but not knowing what to do. When we got home that evening, I told Mom and Dad I wanted to talk to them. I remember clearly my mom praying with me the prayer of salvation. I don't know the exact words we spoke. But I do know that I asked God to forgive me and come into my heart and make me His child. After the prayer, my mother said something that night that made an indelible impression on me. With tears in her eyes, she scooped me up on her lap. She held me close, and she said, "Six years ago

God gave you to us. Tonight, we have to give you back to him."

Never underestimate the power your words have on your children. From that moment on, I knew that my life was not my own. And I knew that I didn't belong to my parents. That sounds a little weird looking back on it in my mid-forties, but I knew from that night that God had a plan and purpose for my life. I did not know exactly what it would be at that point, but I knew that my parents had handed me to God for that purpose. In the story of Samuel, Hannah gave Samuel over to Eli the priest when he was a young boy, to be dedicated to God's service. My parents were giving me over to God's service.

I started looking for what I was called to do. It took me over twenty more years to figure it out, but I knew from that night on that I had a higher purpose. My parents "spoke life" to me that night and I don't even think they knew it. Their words encouraged me to be all that God was calling me to be.

———

I had a recent experience with my mother that reminded me of how my words can affect patients. She had been struggling with some vertigo and sinus issues. She went in to see an otolaryngologist (an ears, nose, and throat doctor), at the same practice as her regular doctor. After a cursory hearing test and a quick exam, the physician said that she "could have a tumor," but she doubted it, and she was going to order an MRI to rule that out. My mother heard NOTHING other than the word tumor. She was devastated and in shock, and could think of nothing else until she could get that radiology test one week later. It turns out she did not have a tumor, but she suffered a week of emotional and mental turmoil thinking that she might.

I wonder how many times I do that. I remember the times I get it right, but I'm sure I forget (with my selective memory) the times I get it wrong.

Yet for all the times I may get it right at work, I so often get it wrong at home. Despite my parents' great example noted above, I still screw it up! Parenting must be one of the most humiliating and humbling experiences on the planet. You quickly realize that all your worst character flaws, especially your words and actions, are bluntly played back for you in your children. My oldest daughter, who is cursed with my genetics, is approaching her teenage years. Three weeks after her twelfth birthday, I was pretty sure there was a demon possession in the house. Intermittently, she started having outbursts of emotional lability that I cannot explain. She was getting ready for school one morning and asked me to put her hair in a ponytail. I did the best job that I could, given the fact she has naturally curly hair that is very fine and wispy. I finished the job, and she turned around to review my work in the full-length mirror in the kitchen (which, by the way, is there so that all the women in the house can inspect themselves before walking out the door). With one glance, she melted into a puddle in the floor, wailing about how I had ruined her life and this was never going to work. Furthermore, I was once again crowned "the worst mother ever."

I tried to interject a few words, such as *I'm sorry* or *I can fix it.* She would hear none of it. She stormed upstairs to her room and slammed the door. I stood there be bewildered, looking at my husband. I exclaimed, "What in the world was that?"

My sweet husband simply smiled, chuckled at me, and said,

"Oh, honey, that was just you!" Ouch. "No worries. I've got this. I've had twenty-five years to practice with you." He went up the stairs, had some sort of intervention, and came down with my daughter back to her adorable, normal self.

Over the last year, I have witnessed several more of these emotional outbursts. What I've had to do, however, is take a long look in the mirror. Where did she learn that behavior? Is it genetic? Now, lest you think I have demonstrated the art of a really good tantrum, complete with lying on the floor and kicking, please know that I have not. However, I do likely express my frustration in equally unhealthy ways, often with my words. My children notice.

One Christmas morning, we were exchanging gifts in our family's traditional way. We tackled the stockings first. Joe and I usually put a small gift in everyone's stocking, and the children have gotten in the habit of putting a little something in our stockings as well. I reached in mine and pulled out what appeared to be a hand-sewn rag doll. I flipped it around to the front and realized this was none other than my very own "Dammit Doll." My husband was bent over double, laughing. I'm sure I had a look of utter shock on my face. I eventually smiled and thanked them for the gift. I then asked, "Who had this lovely idea?"

My kids giggled, and the oldest replied as the spokesperson, "Well, Mom, we were in a gift store with Daddy, and saw the doll and thought of you, since that is your favorite word!" OMG. For those of you who have never seen a Dammit Doll, it is a lovely rag doll with floppy yarn hair. Across the front it has this poem.

> *Whenever things don't go so well,*
> *And you want to hit the wall and yell,*

Here's a little dammit doll,
That you can't do without.
Just grasp it firmly by the legs
And find a place to slam it.
As you whack the stuffing out
Yell "Dammit! Dammit! Dammit!"

For the record, I haven't said dammit, at least in my children's midst, since then. But I have done some soul searching. I realized that my words muttered under my breath do not go unnoticed. And I was doing a lousy job of teaching my kids about the importance of speaking life.

I was beginning to think that I was cured of my potty mouth until I was once again busted by my children. I was on an early morning conference call that I had to take while simultaneously serving breakfast to my crew. As usual, the kitchen became a little loud, and I wandered off to the bedroom as their dad took over serving. Within a few minutes, I heard bloodcurdling screams from the kitchen and lots of crying. I decided to let Dad handle the situation and finish my call. I went on to work, and at about eight fifteen, I received a call from my husband on my work phone (he knew I would not answer the cell). His greeting was, "Honey, you have a problem."

I had no idea what he was referring to. He then asked if I had heard the crying in the kitchen earlier. Of course I had, and so had most of the neighbors as well! He explained that Tattie had reached into the refrigerator to get her lunch at the same time that Trilla had opened the freezer door to get her ice pack. As Tattie stood up, she slammed her head on the freezer door and fell to the ground in tears. As this was happening, my husband was standing at the counter, helping to pack lunches with the boys, then six years old. Tyre, without missing a beat or looking up, said under his breath, "When Mommy does that, she says, 'Shit.'" Joe thought he misheard him, so he asked Tyre to repeat what he'd said. Tyre shrugged his shoulders and looked at Joe. "Well, when my mom hits her head, she says, 'Shit.'" Yikes! Busted again.

> *From the same mouth come blessing and cursing.*
> *My brothers, these things ought not to be so.*

James 3:10 (English Standard Version)

I'm working on it. I'm trying to find better words to use when frustrated. I'm seeking to speak life instead of cursing.

But I'm not a total screw up; I did have a moment of affirmation recently with the boys. Every night, I pray for my kids and tuck them in. Why do I do that? Because I still can! I know they'll outgrow it eventually, but I'm not ready for that yet. (And they aren't either. My middle-schooler was up late working on a homework assignment on the family computer in the kitchen. I prayed for her there and headed off to bed. About thirty minutes later, she appeared at the door of my room because she had not gotten her hug and kiss goodnight. She wanted that blessing.)

With the boys' evening prayers, I have ended every one with a reminder that they were not only loved, but they were *chosen* for this family. They always giggle and tell me they love me more than I love them, and then we go back and forth with "No, I love you more" for several rounds.

Just a few months ago, I was praying for Tyre and tucking him in and he said, "Mom, I feel so sorry for my sisters."

I had no idea what he was referring to. I assumed they'd had some disagreement during the day or that he felt sorry for them for being girls. I asked him to explain.

"Well, Titus and I were chosen for this family. They just happened to come out of your belly. You didn't choose them."

Wow! He knows he was chosen for this family. I hope he always feels that way. I did not think it was the right time to explain that his sisters were sent here from heaven as well. I just smiled and assured him that he, indeed, was chosen.

Words. They have the power of life in them.

15

Leaning In

*Come to me all who are weary. . . . For my yoke is easy
and my burden is light.*

Matthew 11:28, 30

I had breakfast recently with the head of human resources for
the second-largest nonprofit health-care organization in United
States. I was quite honored to be invited to breakfast with "my boss,"
and I really did not know the agenda of the meeting. I was not sure
she knew exactly what leadership role I served within this behemoth
organization, so I found myself explaining my job to her. At some
point in the conversation, she asked me a question that really made
me think: "You're a woman, you're a mom, you're a doctor, and
you're an administrator. Whether you like it or not, people listen to
you. So, what is it you want to be doing with your life right now? Are
you going to pull away, or are you going to lean in?"

After a few hours of soul-searching, I really believe I'm exactly
where God wants me and I'm doing exactly what I'm supposed to

be doing. I have the awesome privilege to shepherd other physicians along this road of health-care change. I am the director of internal medicine for my organization, which is huge! As of 2016, we have over 1800 physicians and over 700 advanced clinical practitioners (such as physician assistants or nurse practitioners), working in 200 physician groups or practices in over 600 locations. And we care for over 1 million unique patients. Yes, it's big job and a daunting responsibility.

I came to this role as administrator with great reluctance. Just as I never thought of myself as a mother or a doctor when I was growing up, I certainly never thought of myself as a health-care administrator. But when I step into this role every week, it feels like I am putting on a pair of well-worn slippers. It just fits.

This journey started about ten months after the boys came home. An opportunity came across my desk to take a newly created position as a physician leader in Internal Medicine for the network where I practice. At that point, health-care reform was all over the news, but we had not yet coined the term *Obamacare*. I was just starting to get comfortable as a physician taking care of patients and feeling like I knew what I was doing. Malcolm Gladwell, in the book *Outliers*, talks about the concept of needing ten thousand hours of practice in a field to achieve mastery. At that point in my career, I was about eight years into being a doctor, which is about ten thousand hours. I was feeling like I knew how to be physician.

I could see the tsunami of change on the horizon, and I thought it would be much better to be sitting at the table helping to inform the decisions made about what I did for the next twenty years than sitting on the back row waiting to have something done to me. I certainly did not have a huge margin of time in my schedule, with four kids under the age of six, but I wanted to be part of the solution that made my job sustainable. So I threw my hat in the ring and found myself entering the world of health-care administration. Over the last eight years, that role has expanded and morphed into the Director of Internal Medicine for Carolinas HealthCare System Medical Group. It is second in size only to the VA as a not-for-profit health-care-providing entity. This role is total chaos, but it is exhilarating!

My role is one with many facets. First and foremost, I am a team builder. I have the amazing opportunity to get to know the physicians and providers at multiple practices, and to determine what are the biggest obstacles impeding their delivery of care to patients. I try to connect them with resources within our huge organization to make their jobs better. I get to share best practices of various physicians trying to sort out the demands placed on us. I remind physicians that we are working toward the goal of taking great care of our patients while still meeting the demands of health-care change. The only constant in medicine is change!

When I finished my residency, as was the experience of most of my colleagues, the hardest thing about my job was figuring out which antibiotic to order for a community-acquired pneumonia, or how to treat a simple muscle strain of the back or ankle. In the field of internal medicine, you are trained to be a hospitalist. That means that the majority of your training takes place in an inpatient setting, taking care of the sickest of the sick patients in the hospital. Many are sedated and require interventions only available in a hospital. Therefore, when I finished my residency training, I was pretty good at managing a ventilator or a drip of vasopresser medications for a hemodynamically unstable patient, but I knew very little about outpatient medicine.

So if you presented to me a simple sinusitis, I was frantically searching the books (yes, books back then, as online clinical reference material was just coming to the forefront of medicine; I had been exposed to several web-based medical tools for providers, including UpToDate, Medscape, and Epocrates, but their use in the daily practice of medicine was far from commonplace). As with many things in life, I learned by doing. My patients were, and are, my greatest teachers. Even now, not a day goes by when I don't have to admit that I don't know something. Every time I walk into an exam room, I get to start over. There is a new presentation of disease that I have the awesome opportunity to decipher. I learn something new about how we are fearfully and wonderfully made every time.

As I was learning so much about being a doctor, I faithfully documented what I observed and processed. Believe it or not, it was paper-and-pencil based. Or, at least dictated onto a paper chart. I understood the concept that if you didn't document it, it didn't happen. I got pretty good at it over the first few years. Then there was a huge disrupter—the electronic medical record. I was already pretty computer savvy in my non-professional world, with two smart devices in my purse. But that electronic reality had not entered my professional career.

Over the first few years of my leadership role, I had the task of transitioning my colleagues from a completely paper-based system to a paperless one, wherein every interaction with our patients—

from writing prescriptions to documenting a visit to billing—was done on a computer screen. Let me tell you, trying to teach a seventy-year-old internist that new trick was not easy! I have a few scars and bruises to prove it. I heard every argument in the book about how using standard documentation templates and voice recognition software would "ruin" the personal touch of medicine and be fraught with errors. Yet we pressed on.

The unintended consequence of digitizing information was that we could quantify data in ways that had never been possible before. Over the next few years, we started realizing that what we thought we were doing with our patients was probably not reality. It is easy for a physician to say that he or she "always" ordered appropriate preventive care for a patient (such as a mammogram or a colonoscopy). But once the data was searchable, we realized that we were doing a terrible job. In 2003, McGlynn et al. published a famous study in the *New England Journal of Medicine* indicating that only 55 percent of patients in the United States received the health care recommended by evidence-based medicine.[16] RAND Researchers released another report in 2006, further leveraging computer-generated data that supported this conclusion.[17] With the ability of electronic tracking, we were able to see, for the first time, the quality of care we were delivering.

With technology, we came to the realization of how inefficient we were and how much waste there was in health care. The emergence of this data was impetus for what we now call health-care

16 McGlynn et al., "The Quality of Health Care Delivered to Adults in the United States," *New England Journal of Medicine* 348, no. 26 (2003): 2635–2645.
17 "The First National Report Card on the Quality of Health Care in America," *RAND Health*, 2006.

reform. I won't lie and say I'm a huge fan of the Affordable Care Act. From a provider standpoint, it really is not health-care reform at all. It is thousands of pages of regulation on payment reform. We know that the health care we provide is expensive; we just need to figure out how to be less expensive without compromising care and quality.

Let me tell you, seeing your data and how you measure up to new regulations for the first time can be a humbling experience. Believe me, I've had many "lively conversations" with my colleagues over how the data just does not lie!

Over the last eight years, however, we've made great progress. We have been able to effect change and see tangible differences in metrics around cancer screenings and diabetes management. Just recently, I had the opportunity to share with the leadership of our organization that of the almost sixty thousand diabetics we manage, their care ranks in the top decile nationally! Yes, top 10 percent! We have been able to create processes and standard work around things that we all knew we should be doing as physicians. We have been able to leverage technology to give us the data to know what we need to do better. The work is invigorating.

We are starting to understand that medicine is a team sport. Gone are the days of an intimate interaction between a provider and a patient. In order to provide the care that our patients need, we need to learn to act like teams. Talk about a paradigm shift! Most physicians, and internists in particular, are trained to be in charge. We are taught that the buck stops with us. It is our clinical acumen that drives patient care. Our medical license is on the line for every decision that we make. Suddenly, we are being asked to relinquish some autonomy and rely on other members of the health-care community to help us take care of patients. Ever tried to initiate a new standard work process in a room with ten control freaks? Welcome to my day, every day!

Management guru Peter Drucker quipped, "Culture eats strategy for breakfast." I have found this to be incredibly sage as I am trying to effect a culture change in the world of health care. All those classes from my master's on social theories, group interactions, and organizational development have come into play. So if you ask me what my job is as a health-care administrator, I'll tell you that I am a cultural change agent, trying to teach my colleagues to learn to delegate and to share responsibility for managing patients and health-care teams. We are reforming how we deliver health care, making it, hopefully, more efficient, more cost-effective, and more patient centered. That drives me. That inspires me. But sometimes, that hurts as well.

I just left the most difficult meeting I've had as a manager in the last several years. It's never happened before, but I actually lost it. No, I didn't pitch a conniption fit, as my dear grandmother would have said. No, I did not yell at anyone. No, I did not spew forth expletives. But I did cry. Not a professional response, and probably not a response I should have displayed in this setting. But I came face-to-face with my own humanity when someone's words really hurt. In fact, they still hurt. And I'm having a hard time fighting back tears as I write this.

I was having a conversation with a provider about performance and about his unwillingness and/or inability to rise to the challenge of quality and patient care standards that are part of the "brave new world" of health-care reform. He lashed out at me, calling me names and degrading my motherhood, my children, and my family. To me this translates as: I cannot do all the things you do, and I'm flat-out jealous that you are figuring out how to manage all these changes. The hurtful words—the anger, the frustration, the finger waved in my face—were not really directed against me. They were aimed at the change that is rolling over us in medicine. But the words still hurt.

Throughout the conversation, though, which continued far beyond when the tears started, I searched for fruits of the Spirit in this person's interactions with me and the other leaders in the room. There were none. No peace, no patience, no kindness, no self-control. Just fear and anger. I know he saw that his words hurt. But I also hope he saw forgiveness and a true desire to help him carry the weight. He was nearing retirement and didn't know what he wanted to do with his life. He couldn't keep up with the pace of seeing multiple patients a day and getting the work done.

Although he could not see it, I was there to help him find a place where he could be productive and fruitful in his last years of practice. He was carrying a huge burden, but he had yet to realize he needed help carrying the yoke. Sometimes, my job as an administrator is as yoke-bearer.

The yoke was a large wooden apparatus that was placed over the neck of at least two oxen. It allowed them to share the burden of plowing, drawing loads, or pulling instruments used for farming. Often, farmers would bind older oxen with younger oxen to help teach the younger oxen how learn the commands of plowing without having to feel the full burden. The older ox would have the tighter brace and carry more of his share until the younger ox "caught on" to the process. The Old Testament uses the term yoke figuratively to refer to slavery, servanthood, oppression, and formed submission. I have often thought of the "burden of health-care reform" as a yoke placed around the necks of physicians and providers. It is a heavy load to bear alone.

In the New Testament (Matthew 11:28–30), Jesus says: "Come to me, all you who are weary and burdened, and I will give you rest. Take my yoke upon you and learn from me, for I am gentle and humble in heart, and you will find rest for your souls. For my yoke is easy and my burden is light."

I don't think Jesus is talking about physical labor here. I think he's talking about the heavy burden of the system of works that the Pharisees placed on the backs of the people of Israel. I look at all the changes in health care and in our industry as similar to all the laws the Pharisees created. The Affordable Care Act alone had 2,700 pages at inception (and has now ballooned to over 20,000 pages) of minuscule regulations that are exhausting. Take, for example, the requirements of "meaningful use" of an electronic medical record. The boxes we have to check to be considered compliant are soul-sucking and provide no value (perceived or real) to the patients. Or, take the new coding requirements called ICD-10. Overnight, all the codes we had memorized from many years of practice became obsolete, and we had to start over. Did you know there is a code for "injury by flying turtle"? (Really, who sat in a government cubicle and thought all this up?) I feel like my job in leadership is to couple myself to my providers and help them carry the load. I may be the younger ox with some of my providers, but I can help my older counterparts "learn the commands" and move forward in tilling the fertile ground of health, wholeness, and healing for every patient with whom we interact.

I tried to do that with the surly doctor described earlier. I am not sure that he got the message. But one boulder in the field is not going to stop me from "leaning in" to the challenge to plow on.

16

Gratitude

"A thief is only there to steal and kill and destroy.
I came so they can have real and eternal life,
more and better life than they ever dreamed of."

John 10:10 (The Message)

I came home from work a few weeks ago on an emotional and spiritual high. I could not wait to tell my family about the amazing blessings and opportunities for sharing grace that I had been given at work. I had seen four patients that day with whom I had the opportunity to pray, to lay hands on them, and to meet them at the point of need with God's grace. It was beautiful. I was just bursting at the seams with thankfulness for the day.

Unfortunately, I walked in my door and Satan slapped me upside the head with joy killers. My substitute nanny (my au pair was out of town) informed me that two of my children were up in their rooms because they had been bickering with their siblings. They were so mean to each other that she did not know what to do, so she just sent them to their rooms. Instead of sharing joy with my kids, I needed to administer discipline. Joy killer number one. Ugh! I have learned over the years that I should not administer discipline in anger, so I decided to cool off before calling the kids downstairs.

I walked into our mudroom/laundry to hang up my purse and realized that my children had not put away their laundry. There were four bins of laundry spilling over onto the floor. Fridays are laundry day. The expected task when you get home from school is to put away your laundry, sometimes with the help of the babysitter or nanny. Since we had a substitute sitter, I had scrambled and stayed up late the night before to get all the loads through the washer and dryer before going to bed. Opportunists that they are, my children had failed to mention to the substitute nanny their normal Friday duties. I guess they assumed that if she did not tell them to do it, they did not have to!

I started toward my bedroom to carry my own laundry and could not get there for the barricade in the middle of my living room. One of my children—and I knew exactly which one— had built a fort three feet high out of ottomans, the piano bench, afghans, and all the cushions off the chairs and couches. I tripped over an afghan and my whole load of laundry fell scattered across the floor. Ugh. Another simple rule I have for my children is that the first floor the house needs to be neat and tidy by five p.m. every day. I love creativity, and I encourage make-believe play. However, "to everything there is a season and a time to every purpose under heaven" (Ephesians 3:1), and the time was 5:20. They knew better. Joy killer number two. This was not helping me cool off.

But I went ahead and called for my children to come downstairs and complete their chores, and I realized they were upstairs playing Wii. Yes, this is another forbidden activity until your chores are done. At this point, expletives were running through my head. I realized that they had completely overrun the sitter. I collapsed the fort with my stomping feet, made my way to my bedroom, and took off my heels, as my feet were begging for mercy at this point in the day. I came back out to the den to assist in cleaning up the mess.

But as I walked barefoot through the den, I stepped in a yellow, soppy circle on my rug. Yep, the dog had peed in the middle of the living room floor! Now, this was not the dog's fault, but the fault of my children who had failed to take her outside. Again, a very simple chore for which they hold responsibility. The dog needs to go out every couple of hours. They had been home for several hours and failed to take the dog on her walk. Well, at that point, I lost it. The expletives floating in my head erupted like a volcano out of my mouth. The high that I had been floating on when I walked in the door had come crashing down. In a matter of five minutes, I had moved from feeling like a great doctor on a mission for God to feeling like a failing parent with my household falling apart. Painful.

And then, joy killer number three showed up. Guilt. You know, that nagging feeling that weasels its way into your soul. All those voices started asking me why I was spending so much time at work, why was I being so selfish pursuing my career, why was I not there shepherding my children? Obviously, my children needed me. The bad-mother script started playing in my head as well. I must be doing something wrong if my children could not get along with each other, could not remember the rules, or do their chores without strict supervision. Rational thinking, no. But honest, gut-wrenching guilt, yes.

I just sat down and cried. I plopped on the couch, wrapped in my blanket of self-pity, and watched as my kids tried dutifully to clean up the cushions, afghans, and puddle of pee. One by one, they crawled up on the couch with me and snuggled in. "We love you, Mommy. We're sorry, Mommy. We'll do better, Mommy." Gradually, I allowed their snuggles to invade my guilt, and God spoke softly to me through their words. Satan had tried to steal my joy through the four beings that should be bearers of my joy. They are kids. They are not perfect. They will eventually grow up. I heard the words of an instructor of a Love and Logic parenting class I had taken ten years before. "Your job as a parent is to raise a responsible thirty-year-old." Well, I guess I still have time!

We got through the evening, family movie night and all, and I settled in to bed to read through my emails and nightly devotion. Sitting in my email was a Twitter feed from my husband. Let me pause and say that I am not sure what my husband does at work, but he seems to have a lot of time to tweet! On any given day, I rarely have time to skip to the loo before one p.m., but he can easily send me three or four emails linking to his favorite tweets. This one, however, got my attention. The link read, "A new study finds the happiest parents are those who have four or more kids." I was intrigued. It was an article in *The Daily Signal* by Leah Jessen. According to the article, a study conducted by Australia's Edith Cowan University found parents had the most life satisfaction with larger families. The study's author, Dr. Bronwyn Harman, "spent five years interviewing hundreds of parents from different family makeups and based her findings on resilience, social support, self-esteem, and life satisfaction. "What is important for kids are things like consistency, boundaries, and [to] know that they are loved, no matter what,'" Harman explained.

Ironically, Harman initially believed parents with more children would be less happy, but her research concluded that the joy parents get from their children balances out the more chaotic family nature than that of a smaller family. Finally, the study showed that children of larger families are more independent at a younger age and always have friends. Well, God knew I needed to hear that! I realized that my "broken boundaries" were okay, that my consistent rules should stand, and that my kids knew they were loved, no matter what. And I was thankful for the chaos and pandemonium. The thankfulness turned my despair into joy.

Gratitude is the tonic for joy stealers. There is good secular research to prove it. Dr. Robert Emmons is the world's leading scientific expert on gratitude. He is a professor of psychology at the University of California, Davis, and the founding editor-in-chief of *The Journal of Positive Psychology.* He is also the author of the books *Gratitude Works!: A 21-Day Program for Creating Emotional Prosperity* and *Thanks! How the New Science of Gratitude Can Make You Happier.* In his work, he and his colleagues have studied thousands of patients of all ages and found consistently positive effects of an attitude of gratitude.

Physically, folks who practice gratitude (in the form of keeping a gratitude journal), are less bothered by aches and pain, exercise more, and take better care of their health, sleep longer, feel more refreshed upon awakening, and have lower blood pressure. Socially, these folks have higher levels of positive emotions, including optimism, happiness, joy, and pleasure, and report feeling more alert, alive, and awake. Psychologically, such individuals are more compassionate and forgiving toward others, are more helpful and generous toward those in need, and are more outgoing—and, thus, less isolated and lonely.

Emmons defines gratitude as having two components:

> First, it's an affirmation of goodness. We affirm that there are good things in the world, gifts and benefits we've received. This doesn't mean that life is perfect; it doesn't ignore complaints, burdens, and hassles. But when we look at life as a whole, gratitude encourages us to identify some amount of goodness in our life.
>
> The second part of gratitude is figuring out where that goodness comes from. We recognize the sources of this goodness as being outside of ourselves. It didn't stem from anything we necessarily did ourselves in which we might take pride. We can appreciate positive traits in ourselves, but I think true gratitude involves a humble dependence on others: We acknowledge that other people—or even higher powers, if you're of a spiritual mindset—gave us many gifts, big and small, to help us achieve the goodness in our lives.[18]

I believe it is the spiritual reality of gratitude that drives the physical, social, and psychological benefits. Joy is derived from a heart full of gratitude. Henry Ward Beecher, the nineteenth-century American clergyman with a sordid past, is quoted as saying: "Gratitude is the fairest blossom that springs from the soul."

The Bible pairs thankfulness with joy throughout the narrative

---

18 Robert Emmons, "Why Gratitude Is Good," *Greater Good: The Science of a Meaningful Life*, November 16, 2010.

of the Scriptures. 1 Thessalonians 5:15 commands us: "Rejoice always, pray continually, *give thanks* in all circumstances; for this is God's will for you in Christ Jesus" (emphasis is mine). The "all circumstances" applies to days like the joy killer described above. It also applies to the days when I have to give a patient bad news, when I have to intervene in a partner's patient complaint, or when I get called at three a.m. for a critical lab value. The Bible says we should be giddy with gratefulness for all He has done in us and through us. We should be drunk on our thankfulness. "Do not get drunk on wine, which leads to debauchery. Instead, be filled with the Spirit, speaking to one another with psalms, hymns, and song from the Spirit. Sing and make music from your heart to the Lord, *always giving thanks* to God the Father for everything, in the name of our Lord Jesus Christ" (Ephesians 5:18-20; emphasis mine). It should be the thankfulness that brings order to the chaos.

Let the peace of Christ rule in your hearts, since as members of one
body you were called to peace. And be thankful. Let the message
of Christ dwell among you richly as you teach and admonish
one another with all wisdom through psalms, hymns, and songs
from the Spirit, singing to God with gratitude in your hearts. And
whatever you do, whether in word or deed, do it in the name of the
Lord Jesus, give thanks to God the Father through him.

Colossians 3:15–17

In this verse is the only instance of the Greek word *rule* in the New Testament. It means to arrange or conduct the contest. It also means to confer the prize or victory. It is similar to the word we use for umpire. Through our thankfulness, we find peace that settles the chaos and brings us back to the rules of the game of life. The thankfulness cannot be extracted from the reality of God's indwelling and his transformation in us. I am not sure Emmons would agree, but I would suggest that it is the specific gratitude for what God does in us that brings true joy. I would be interested to know how many of his study participants knew the peace of God. Just as my seminary professor said that good psychological theories had reflections of God's truth in them, I would say that Emmons's observations about gratitude reflect the attitude God intends all of us to have toward Him.

Melody Beattie, a well-known self-help author, summarizes this reality: Gratitude unlocks the fullness of life. It turns what we have into enough, and more. It turns denial into acceptance, chaos to order, confusion to clarity. It can turn a meal into a feast, a house into a home, a stranger into a friend. Gratitude makes sense of our past, brings peace for today, and creates a vision for tomorrow.

Indeed, life here is maddening. It is exhausting. It is chaos, unfolding around me all the time. There is no control. I've tried. Control is an illusion. I've tried to plan my life, step by step for over forty years. It has not worked. And I am so thankful that it has not gone as I planned it! I'm the woman, wife, mother, doctor, administrator, and hot mess that I never dreamed I could be. I am so thankful for all the insanity. The joy God has brought and continues to bring to my soul is exhilarating. This is real life, and it's better and more full than I could have ever imagined. So, with a heart full of gratitude, I will continue to embrace entropy and find meaning in the joys of motherhood, medicine, and mayhem.

Acknowledgments

First and foremost, I want to thank my Fabulous Family. (They will get the joke.) My precious husband, my soul mate and my best friend, has been the catalyst for making this book a reality. No one has sacrificed more than he in giving me the freedom and encouragement to do this. And I want to thank my brood. My kids just rock. They have been incredibly supportive and patient with me as I wrote this narrative. They have also been quite inspirational. There is never a dearth of content when you are trying to write about the chaos of raising a family! I would be remiss if I did not thank my parents as well. They laid the foundation and continue to ground me. The chaos of my life started with them.

Second, I want to thank the hundreds of people to have directed and redirected my path: schoolteachers, Sunday school leaders, youth ministers, college and seminary professors, preceptors, and friends who have looked me straight in the face and asked tough questions and provided sage advice. Thanks for your patience with me. And thanks for pursuing me when I ran headstrong in the wrong directions! Thanks to my book coach, Betsy Thorpe, for shepherding me through this whole process. I could not have done it without you! Thanks to my editor, Maya Myers, for your grace with a newbie writer. Thanks to my book designer, Diana Wade, whose creative eye made my words look beautiful on the page. And, thanks to my photographer, Mike

Newcomer, who captured my chaos in pictures.

Third, I want to thank my patients. Not a day goes by that I am not humbled and inspired by the resilience of the human body and the human spirit. It is a privilege to serve as your physician.

Finally, I am thankful that the God of the Universe has given me opportunity to share my story. I know, however, it is not my story. It is His. I am honored to be part of His story of redemption in my life and in the lives of those around me. Thank you for this messy life.

About the Author

Carmen Teague, M.D., attended the University of North Carolina at Chapel Hill on the prestigious Morehead-Cain Scholarship, earned a Masters Degree in Counseling from Gordon-Conwell Theological Seminary in Massachusetts, and worked in Alzheimer's disease research at Duke University. She then attended the UNC-Chapel Hill School of Medicine and completed her residency at Carolinas Medical Center in Charlotte, NC, in Internal Medicine. She joined Mecklenburg Medical Group, part of Carolinas HealthCare System, in June of 2004, and now serves as the Director of Internal Medicine for Carolinas HealthCare System Medical Group Division.

She is married to her high-school sweetheart and they have four beautiful children. The girls came by birth; the boys came by plane. All four came by God's grace to her family. She is an avid water-skier, triathlete, and Crossfit fanatic. She serves as a LifeGroup leader at her church and as a medical mission team leader in the community. She enjoys sharing her story with professional and faith-based organizations throughout the Charlotte area. You can follow her blog at *www.carmen-teague.com* and on Facebook at *carmenteagueauthor*.

CPSIA information can be obtained
at www.ICGtesting.com
Printed in the USA
BVHW050534120522
636831BV00004B/10